ONE OF US

A BIOLOGIST'S WALK AMONG BEARS

BARRIE K GILBERT

FriesenPress

Suite 300 - 990 Fort St
Victoria, BC, V8V 3K2
Canada

www.friesenpress.com

First Edition — 2019

Editor: Kaylene Johnson-Sullivan
Photographer: Shea Wyatt

To Jim Thompson, Helicopter Pilot

Grateful acknowledgment to photographers Tom Murphy, Dave Campbell, Shea Wyatt and Owen Nevin.

I would like to recognize many friends and relatives who made contributions. Any errors or misinterpretations are strictly the responsibility of the author.

ISBN
978-1-5255-4850-5 (Hardcover
978-1-5255-4851-2 (Paperback
978-1-5255-4852-9 (eBook

1. NATURE, ANIMALS, WILDLIFE

Distributed to the trade by The Ingram Book Company

For Jim Thompson
For forty-two extra years

Contents

PART 4

Science Meets Politics: Wilderness Values, Bears' Future

PART 5

Imperatives from the Past

Acknowledgements

Much of this book is based on research done over many years with continuous financial support from the National Park Service and U.S. Forest Service as well as in-kind use of facilities and accommodations generously provided by Dean Wyatt, the former owner of Knight Inlet Lodge. I am especially grateful to former resource biologist Kathy Jope and the superintendents at Katmai National Park.

If I began to recognize and thank all the people who inspired and encouraged me to write, I would be off on another odyssey. Luckily, no one told me not to mess with a mammal whose flight-or-fight response involves lawyers, because the grizzly bear has all the advantages. The analytical minds of lawyers, with their use of the best science, often come to the rescue of bear conservation (and justice for some people who are injured when grizzly management falls short). I am grateful to many environmental lawyers.

I would like to thank the following people, in no particular order: Peter Klopfer, Carl Safina, Jim Halfpenny, Jesse Logan. Paul Paquet, Chris Genovali, Brian Horejsi, Dean Wyatt, Owen Nevin, David Morris, Lance Craighead, Kaylene Johnson-Sullivan, Kathy Brew, Doug Peacock, Louisa Willcox, Ray Bane, Jim Thompson, Denis Sizemore, Wayne McCrory, Ian McAllister, Steve Stringham, Mary Meagher,

Danielle Chi, Anne Braaten, Rick Bass, Anthony Crupi, Dave Sheppard, Don Dumond, Bruce Hastings, Jonathan Kingdon, Michelle McLellan, Tom Murphy, Steve Primm, Bonnie Rice, Susan Clark, Arthur Morris, Larry Roy, Bill Samuel, David Mattson, Todd Wilkinson, Andrew Wright, George Wuerthner.

This book benefitted immensely from the loving criticism of my wife, Katherine Gilbert. Any limitations remain solely mine.

Introduction

I don't really know bears at all. But then, does anybody? My first up-close grizzly encounter took place by surprise on a mountain ridge in northwest Yellowstone National Park, and it left me nearly dead ten miles from the nearest road. The bear so resented my intrusion that she tore half my face off with one bite. I was rescued, hospitalized, reconstructed, recovered, and given a chance to spend the rest of my career spying on other grizzlies, who were much more accommodating.

In my office, I have file folders on four bear naturalists who were killed by bears. Some were friends. They worked closely with wild grizzly bears most of their adult lives: one in Alaska, one in the Yukon, and two in Kamchatka, in eastern Russia.

My experience with grizzlies has parallels with another killer of experts: avalanches. No matter how well prepared and skillful you are, in time, a situation will arise that can get you. I have always had a healthy respect for bears (and real fear when their behavior commands it). I have never suffered from the sympathetic fallacy, that bears will return affection if I love them. That was true even before I had a field course in stark reality: bites that required over nine hundred sutures as the medics reconstructed various parts of my body. Far beyond ideas and concepts, I discovered nothing is as real as having a bear tear pieces off you.

In September 1978, a year after that accident, I was off capturing black bears in Yosemite National Park with my grad student, Bruce Hastings. Five years later, I began behavioral studies on brown bears in Katmai National Park, Alaska, among the planet's largest bears. This book chronicles my "to hell and back" story with grizzlies and why I became a champion of grizzly bears, their habitat, and conservation even after I took a beating from one.

PART 1

Recovery and on to the Nature of the Grizzly

1

A Mauling and a Mountaintop Rescue

We sighted our first grizzlies at 6:04 a.m. on June 27, 1977.

The day had begun with sunlight chasing a long shadow across an alpine lake far below. We were in the Gallatin River headwaters of northwest Yellowstone National Park, 9,900 feet above sea level. Sitting at the top of the world, my graduate student, Bruce, and I were high with excitement as we watched a mother grizzly and three cubs amble toward a small herd of grazing elk. It was late spring in Montana's Gallatin Range. The high valleys were greening up, and the long snowdrifts were melting away.

Only a week earlier, we had left Utah State University to begin a study of grizzly bear responses to backcountry hikers and outfitters on packhorses. Finally, bears were in sight, not too far from the well-used Fawn Pass Trail.

The day before, we had hiked from Indian Creek campground, where we loaded up our gear and headed off into the cool, fresh air of

America's most glorious park. Our pace was swift. We had ten miles to go, packing forty-pound loads across rivulets cutting through sagebrush and mud, soon to become dust.

Toward evening, we crested Bighorn Pass. The sun was down, but the solstice twilight lingered as we made camp. Our campsite was well off the trail near a cliff; we were thinking "grizzly" the entire time. Bruce and I pulled dead branches and snags around the tent, thinking it would slow any inquisitive bear and give us time to collect our wits.

Earlier in the week, we had backpacked to low hills overlooking the bison meadows of Pelican Valley for a study site but had come up dry. A canoe trip down Yellowstone Lake to a trout-spawning stream showed more promise: lots of tracks, scats, and fish pieces but no open ground or high spots to observe bears. Still, I loved the remoteness and access by canoe, mostly for aesthetic reasons. In hindsight I envisioned a dream project: research attempting to solve a bear behavior problem that required canoeing deep into the wilderness. A dreamy delusion would be a better description. Separating useful science from preserving wild country has always conflicted me.

Yellowstone offers unique opportunities to see ecological and evolutionary processes closer to pristine conditions than anywhere in the lower forty-eight, including how the behavior of individual animals fits in. This behavioral observation approach was working in Africa with gorillas and lions, so why not here? Bruce and I shared an interest in animal behavior and psychology as well as woodcraft that would shine later. Bruce was new to the Rockies and cold-water canoeing, but he made up for it with outdoor skills learned in the woods of north Georgia and boundless enthusiasm. His only reticence was canoeing through lightning storms in an aluminum canoe, a bit of wisdom that I failed to fully acknowledge. Lightning strikes can fry a paddler in a metal canoe, another easy way to die in Yellowstone.

We paddled through six thunderstorms, including lightning, hail, rain, and cold fronts that forced us ashore many times. Choppy waves big enough to capsize our canoe forced us to land and huddle under our sturdy vessel. No sooner did each grey-black thunderhead pass than the sun lured us onto the frigid lake once again. This was signature weather in high lakes in the Rockies. We needed another place better suited to see hikers and grizzlies together.

From Bighorn Pass we watched a female with three cubs threaten a big male by chasing him off when he got too close. My notes read, "Cubs stayed very close to female, often at her head, may be feeding on roots dug by mom." The cubs would be seeking security, wary of the big male, a potential cub killer. Much later I realized the male might also have primed a hair-trigger response in the mother toward me.

We watched those bears for almost two hours until they turned uphill into the timber. Hoping to see them closer, I decided to circle far around and above the family. We left the campsite to hike up the backside of Crowfoot Ridge, emerging on top. There was no trail, just stunted trees. We bushwhacked through fallen snags and heavy tree cover, likely a place nobody but Sheep-Eater Indians or Shoshones had ever stepped.

Near the top of the ridge, we emerged into a more open alpine area. Leaving Bruce behind for a nature call, I continued ahead, moving briskly over the ridge to avoid being detected by the elk below. I was worried they would bark in alarm if they saw movement against the skyline. I was not even thinking grizzlies, assuming bears would not be at that elevation (9,200 feet).

Bent over and moving over the ridge, I heard an explosive woof and looked up to see a mass of brown fur launch toward me. With milliseconds to react, I faced an insanely furious grizzly, head down, ears back, and roaring. Low to the ground, her body rocketed toward me. I saw her claws raking the bedrock as she accelerated. I knew this was trouble, not a bluff charge. I had to get out of there. Standing to face her never even entered my mind. This was the furious behavior of a mother protecting her cubs. Later I realized that my fast, low approach probably appeared like I was attacking her. In a state of terror, my only thought was to get away from her.

She caught me in seconds and knocked me face down. Her teeth felt like a row of pick-axes scraping across my head as she tore my scalp off. Strangely, I remember no pain despite the furrow that her tooth carved into my skull.

I turned over to fight her off with my fists. Her second bite came down on my face, a big canine tooth punching into my left eye socket. *This is how you die,* I thought as I felt bones crunch. One bite removed my cheekbone and sinus, exposing brain membranes. I remember clearly, just before that bite, that her breath smelled rotten, like the bottom of a garbage can on a summer day.

As my life drained onto the ground, I went limp, and the biting stopped. Just then Bruce came over the rise, saw the bear standing on me, and yelled "HAAAA!" as loud as he could.

The bear moved off. Her bloody footprints were later tracked going down the mountain.

Within one hour, eight emergency medical technicians—smoke jumpers from the West Yellowstone Hotshot base—and a helicopter pilot carried out a flawless rescue. While standing nearby, Jim Thompson, the enterprising helicopter pilot, took a series of color slides of the rescue with my camera. These proved useful later for rescue training by the National Park Service (NPS).

What the behavior and jaws of an angry grizzly bear can do in less than thirty seconds was described in a report by the attending physicians.

> The injuries included multiple lacerations across the back of the scalp with avulsion of most of the scalp forward to the face. The left side of the face was destroyed, left eye missing, entire lateral aspect left mouth open, all salivary glands of left face destroyed, the left superior nasal and inferior orbit open. In addition, the right eye was compromised with decreased vision.

> Multiple lacerations were present on the chest, abdomen, and upper extremities. The right and left ears were partially avulsed and the left zygoma partially destroyed.
>
> Estimated blood loss was 2/5 of his total volume. Six thousand ml. intravenous fluid were immediately administered before improved vascular conditions existed.

Despite blood loss and wounds requiring close to one thousand sutures, the rescue unfolded in a stunning series of actions. Luckily, we had packed in a handheld radio. My first raspy words to Bruce came from my throat, as my lips were somewhere over by my ear. "Call park headquarters," I gargled. Being twenty minutes by air from headquarters in Mammoth meant a helicopter dispatch would reach us soon.

Upon receiving Bruce's alarming message, "Barrie Gilbert has been attacked by a grizzly," park communications shut down all other transmissions to keep our connection open.

In three days, the park was due to have two new helicopters brought in for firefighting. I had just missed that bus, but I was so lucky to have a pilot with Jim's skill and experience.

Before we lifted off for the flight to Yellowstone's Lake Clinic, I insisted that the bear that I had surprised not be destroyed. I knew this collision was triggered by my sudden appearance and felt that the grizzly should not be a victim of our accidental contact.

A medical clinic nearby in Yellowstone Park might not appear to be a first-rate site for emergency care for such severe trauma, but the dice rolled my way again. Lake Clinic, a huge, sprawling, old complex, had just the medical team needed. Almost unbelievable to me still is that this small clinic had rotated in a team of surgeons with Vietnam field trauma experience. I imagine that dealing with dangling patches of skin and an eyeball jutting out might have been simpler than dealing with shrapnel damage to an army grunt.

After the team stabilized me, the next thing I remembered was ambulance sirens screaming as we careened past traffic to the airport at West Yellowstone. Positioned on the runway was a surgical evacuation unit flown in from the University of Utah Medical School, not far from my home in northern Utah. There I underwent eleven hours of repair, which, I learned later, exhausted their supply of suture material. Within days a new group of senior residents came on board to deliver plastic and reconstructive surgery at its innovative best.

I could fill another book with hospital lore, but I will just tell a story about my lead surgeon, the late Earl Z. Browne. I fell in love with the guy. What impressed me most was the way he seemed to bring me on to the recovery team. Yes, I realized it was probably a ploy to get me over the shock, but his highly personal approach got me over more than one hump. One incident will illustrate.

During a consultation of how my cheek was surviving the rebuilding process, including a puck-shaped pad of plaster in my cheek to keep the transplant flexible, he showed me a slide. It was my face before the suturing began. All my facial skin and scalp was pinned out like a rat dissection in Biology 101. To be honest, I wasn't repelled, but it all seemed so extreme. So, I asked Dr. Browne if he had seen this kind of damage before. His response was classic, a forever memory. "Well, yes," he said, "but not all on the same guy!"

What about the behavior of the bear after it neutralized me? The moment Bruce yelled from behind a bush, the grizzly left me and went downhill and out of sight. Having subdued me, the immediate threat, perhaps a need to return to her cubs and not deal with another person won out. Since the attack was not predatory, there was little likelihood that she would revert to feeding on me. I was unsure about this at that moment though and told Bruce to get up any nearby tree. He assured me the bear was gone.

The news media loves a bear attack. Victims of a grizzly mauling attract a lot of attention. My fifteen minutes of fame came with some media manipulation. A flurry of outdoor writers and TV producers contacted me for interviews, starting at my hospital bed. The storyline they wanted was the usual drama: vicious bear attack, lurid details of injuries, finishing with intrusive probes into raw emotional fallout. I found this exploitive, invasive, and thoughtless. One final indignity came when a Montana photographer stuck her camera in my face when I had removed my glasses, which had an eyepatch attached. Her editor published a story, front page, with a close-up of my disfigured one-eyed face. True to form, the newspaper did not ask my permission to publish the picture. My education was gaining momentum.

These experiences convinced me to deflect questions about my encounter toward an appeal for a more sympathetic perception of grizzlies. Enough of the stereotypes: rogue killers in the woods eager to eat your children. I was fine when they drilled down on why I returned to tracking grizzlies. But when interviews drifted to the seriousness of my injuries conflicting with a return to bears, I pointed to early humankind's history of accommodation with this wilderness native. Even more mysterious to me was the level of credibility they assigned to my knowledge about safety around bears due to the fact I had survived a horrific mauling and then returned to bear research. No one ever challenged my credibility despite my flunking the bear safety course. However, being anointed "bear expert" was useful in talks for breaking the ice. I asked my audiences if they would also attend a lecture on seamanship by Captain Joe Hazelwood of the doomed Exxon Valdez. That ploy worked well to allay their ambivalence or anxiety.

2

Rescue and Recovery

As the years passed, I realized I knew almost nothing about the flight off Crowfoot Ridge that summer morning. Thirty-three years later, the chopper pilot, Jim Thompson, tracked me down by email and gave me the following riveting account.

> Here are a few of the details I remember about our adventure together in 1977. These issues are as fresh in my memory as if they happened yesterday. I think that is because that day was the most dynamic eight hours of flying I have ever experienced. That includes two helicopter combat tours of duty in Viet Nam from 1968 to 1972. Keep in mind that the helicopter we used was not ideal for the job in the first place, and the turbo charger was in the process of failing. The adrenalin meter in my brain was showing max full for the entire day.
>
> My family was grocery shopping in Gardner, Montana when the first call from Bruce came over the radio. We scrambled

back to the park headquarters and discovered the ground crew were in the last phases of attaching the Stokes litter to the helicopter -that tourist class accommodation you spoke of.

Tom Black deserves all the credit for locating you and Bruce so quickly. He had extensive knowledge of the Bighorn Pass and a very clear idea in his mind about on which spur ridge you and Bruce would probably be located. I simply followed his directions and we flew directly to the spot. Also, credit Bruce for being clear-headed and concise in his description of what happened and where.

I tried several times to land the helicopter on the ridge thinking being at the same elevation as you would allow us to get back to Lake much quicker. The wind velocity was greater than 20 MPH gusting to over 35 MPH (possibly higher) and swirling from all directions, seemingly at the same time. After what seemed a long time and too many dangerous attempts to land, Tom and I agreed that the meadow to the North and a few hundred feet lower than the ridge would be the only safe place to land, and we would certainly require the assistance of some other resource. That turned out to be eight smokejumpers who were also highly qualified paramedics and the R4D piloted by one of the most qualified DC3 pilots in the country, Whitey Hawkmeister. By the time we landed, Tom was halfway through a pack of smokes. At one time he had two going at the same time. His adrenalin was also flowing freely.

Tom got out of the helicopter before I could shut the thing down. He instructed me to carry the 12 gauge shot gun and the Stokes litter up the hill. He ran up that hill carrying the medical bag and his .357. Keep in mind, I had spent nearly all my life below 1000' MSL. And here I was at just under 9000' MSL, if my memory serves. Before I was one-quarter of the way up, I began to taste blood and had no idea what was going on. The physician at Lake explained later that it was due to the alveoli in my lungs not adapting sufficiently to the partial pressure of oxygen at that elevation, and they suffered mild rupture. He said I would live.

Tom started an IV in your foot at the direction of the Lake doctor. I took your blood pressure and reported 120/80 over the radio. The communication system at Yellowstone was the best I had ever seen and it contributed greatly to the success of our rescue. I am not a medical person, but figuring out how to take blood pressure just seemed to come to me. Taking pictures with your camera was a reflexive activity. I was fairly experienced with 35mm shooting and just got lucky that the images were in focus and had descent exposure. I thought at the time that a hard history of what we were trying to do might someday come in handy. I am happy that it did. You probably do not remember this: you managed to tell me that I was leaning too heavily on your leg and you would appreciate it if I could relocate. I will never understand how you managed to get that information out to me in your apparent condition. Bruce didn't just stand around idly during all of this activity. He covered your head with his shirt, I think, to ward off the insects and any dirt that might blow onto your wounds. I thought he was very cool-headed and quite helpful.

Tom, Bruce and I soon agreed that the three of us would never be able to safely carry you to the helicopter. The slope seemed to be greater than 40 degrees down a very rugged surface. Tom advised the park headquarters that we needed help. The jump center at West Yellowstone Airport must have been on alert for this possibility as it just seemed like a few minutes before I heard the roar of those big radial engines coming low over the higher ridge just to the west. They made several passes over Crowfoot Ridge assessing the advisability of a jump directly to the ridge. Once again, that would have saved lots of time, but it just couldn't be due to the wind and turbulence. The bundles of materials needed by the jumpers and the rest of us were dropped on the ridge with little effort. Parachutes have much less steer-ability than the helicopter had so the men decided not to try the same landing spot. The eight jumpers were soon climbing up the steep hill after a safe landing in the meadow where the helicopter was sitting. Those well-conditioned men didn't seem to mind the steep climb at all.

I watched in amazement the professionalism of the smoke jumpers. They quickly determined the best course of action for stabilizing you and transporting you to the helicopter. That trip down the hill is what you remember; four jumpers carried you, four carried the supplies. Tom, Bruce and I brought up the rear after securing the site. The smoke jumpers knew as much as I did about that helicopter and how to attach items to it. Preparing the equipment for flight went very smoothly.

The first indication that the trip to Lake might be a little out of the normal flight envelop came when we first lifted off and your side of the machinery wanted to stay on the ground. Ordinarily, for the Bell 47, in Stokes litter application, there needs to be a counter balance of an equal weight on the other side. That was not available for us. On the way to Lake, Tom had to sit almost on my lap to make the helicopter's lateral center-of-gravity come even close to the normal range. Every time Tom slid over to your side to check on you, the helicopter rolled into an un-commanded right-hand turn. Then, when he returned to my lap we were able to fly straight and level again. Turns to the left were almost impossible. It was circus in nature. I don't remember that the smoke jumpers administered a tranquilizing shot, but Tom said you seemed well adjusted to the circumstances.

The landing at Lake was quite a bounce because the old turbo charger was just about one-half gone. Pilotage was also a problem at the time. Tom told me you flinched some on contact. I was afraid there had been some damage to you or the helicopter. Fortunately, everything stayed together. You were rushed into the hospital and from that time on I have very little information concerning your treatment and recovery. I can only thank God that you did recover and you eventually returned to your work. Tom and I were fed and we rested a little. The doctor advised that my bleeding from the lungs is normal in low landers who exert themselves at those higher elevations. That's some way to find out.

We returned to the Bighorn where I was asked to transport all of the smoke jumpers and their gear back to West Yellowstone. None of them wanted that eight-hour hike. Tom and Bruce sat there in the meadow for several hours while I got everyone and everything returned to the airport. At two-at-a-time and a forty-minute round trip it seemed to take forever. I also had to refuel the helicopter one time. Tom, Bruce and I got back to the park headquarters just about in time for supper and a much needed night's sleep.

> You probably did not realize that the helicopter service my charter company provided was the only one in the park until July, so we had little choice in the matter. My personal limitations were just about reached on that second day. Two turbine powered helicopters showed up on July 1 to support the firefighting efforts in the park over the next two months.
>
> I hope this recount of the events of June 27, 1977 will help fill in some of the gaps in information. I will never forget that day. I think that is a function of the amount of adrenalin that was flowing. There are days from Viet Nam I will never forget for the same reason. I hope I haven't worn you out with all of this. I have no knowledge of Tom Black. However, I do recall what friendly help he gave in getting us settled in the park and during the daily flying assignments. I have met several other pilots who worked with Tom and appreciated him as much.

After two months in the hospital, I headed home. (Bruce went to Yosemite National Park for a substitute thesis project on black bears, which I describe in a later chapter.) Fortunately, my objective in Yellowstone, to define grizzly responses to people on trails, was adopted by a young student, Kerry Gunther, who did his observations of Pelican Valley grizzlies and hikers from a nearby mountaintop for his master's thesis. He went on to a successful career with the park as a supervisory bear manager.

In summer 1978, my return to Yosemite found me sitting beside a five-hundred-pound male black bear coming out of anesthesia from our darting project. While pouring cool water over the sleepy monster, I conjured various scenarios of what would happen when it recovered that included flashbacks of my mauling. Bruce had gone off to other tasks. Alone, I rationalized good outcomes, so I was fine as the bear stumbled off safely. Staying with recovering bears is essential, because other bears may attack a handicapped animal.

The huge bear had run off fast when hit by the dart. We chased him as fast as we could, sending his massive bulk up a big ponderosa pine like a cat up a pole, claws raking deep grooves into the bark. I could only imagine the strength of those shoulders and legs when I cut puny slices in the bark with a Bowie knife.

We backed way off to allow the bear to climb down unhindered as the drug took effect, so he would not fall and injure himself. Then we processed him and watched him waddle groggily into the forest.

Fear of that bear was not an issue for me, but I could only guess why. Maybe long experience with animals and my short dose of terror carried the day. Being otherwise risk-averse, such as when I outfitted my first car, a VW beetle, with shoulder belts that would work for smash-up derbies, I wrote off my trauma like a person kicked by a horse might do. But I did have anger issues and some diagnosed PTSD symptoms as I recovered with major facial disfigurement. Suffice to say that I chose to see the staring responses of others as their problem. After all, many people are burdened with mental trauma worse than mine, though it's not visible. I had the advantage of mature age and a supportive family. After a period of administrative mauling by my university, too byzantine to address here, I carried on with my same personality and rejoiced that my hands worked just fine. I was a handsome guy and still am (inside).

PART 2

Grizzly Bear Behavior: Myths, Reality, and Lessons Learned

3

Bears as Adversary

Lewis and Clark Meet Grizzlies

When Clovis people migrated from Asia thirteen thousand years ago, they entered a pristine continent un-impacted by humans. Novel plants and animals made foraging and adapting to winter dependent on rapid learning. The grizzly bear, another hunter-gatherer, based its adaptations of learned traits, good memory, and passing on survival tactics to their young. There was much to learn. Recent research of the broad diet in grizzly foraging, including over one thousand plant and animal species, reveals intriguing ways that might have benefitted Clovis explorers, parallel patterns in the human-bear relationship. Did these primal people benefit from observing grizzlies? Our growing appreciation of grizzlies' intelligence and their cultural adaptations for finding food suggest reasons why early people would watch and mimic bears. But where can we search for records of the earliest responses of grizzlies to people?

A key goal of my research was to uncover grizzly bear behavior that might make their interactions with people more compatible. Studying trail encounters in parks looked promising. Before I share what I learned, let's take a short side trip to explain how direct observation of grizzlies and hikers might contribute.

Coming from an academic tradition that stressed reliable descriptions of behavior in natural environments, I was following Fraser Darling, who wrote *A Herd of Red Deer*, and W.H. Thorpe's *Learning and Instinct in Animals*. My graduate studies on social behavior of semi-wild fallow deer strengthened my perception that the variability, richness, and complexity of mammalian behavior required resolute attention to detail. This approach promised insights into adaptability and learning, leading to better management of people-wildlife conflicts.

In Yellowstone the grizzly bears studied by John and Frank Craighead were captured, collared, and tracked using radio signals. This resulted in new information on basic ecology and habitat use but left gaps in terms of individual behavior. When these bears were protected in 1975 under the Endangered Species Act, the objectives of the federal grizzly team emphasized estimating population size, a direction further yet from understanding the detailed information about differences in behavior of individuals that is fundamental to managing conflicts on backcountry trails and roadside encounters. Thus, a behavioral approach was our goal, a more direct focus on hikers' responses to bears and vice versa.

To gather quantitative data efficiently, we needed to find sites where encounters were predictable. The Craighead brothers took advantage of traditional bear concentrations at dumps, where hundreds of habituated individuals were rewarded by delicious garbage, a cornucopia of hotel leftovers dumped from compactor refuse trucks. However, studying such food-conditioned grizzlies, thoroughly habituated to people, did not yield much useful information on the behavior of wild bears. Were other sites available?

Bruce Hastings and I wanted to monitor trails in Yellowstone's backcountry. Our plan was to determine habitat use by grizzlies with and without people present to see how increasing use of the backcountry might be impacting the growing but precarious grizzly population. The study needed a baseline of natural behavior to compare with bears whose behavior had been changed by people, whether through culling by Yellowstone rangers, the availability of campground food, or even research captures. I also wanted to find accounts of bears that were naïve to armed people, so I turned to historical records documenting first contacts. That search was an eye-opener.

For reliable information on bear behavior before settlement, the diaries of Lewis and Clark proved a reliable source. I reviewed every account mentioning grizzly bears in their journals. Lewis and Clark were among the first European explorers to contact grizzly bears and the first to accurately describe their experiences with "this terrible beast" along the Missouri and Yellowstone Rivers.

My research uncovered a fascinating story, providing new insights about grizzly behavior prior to an era of decimation by poisoning, trapping, and shooting. Could this shed new light on the uncertainty about our earliest contact with North America's biggest terrestrial carnivore?

The *Journals of the Expedition of Discovery* are extraordinarily credible in contrast to the well-spun folklore about encounters with real and imagined grizzlies in pre-settled North America. The careful, voluminous descriptions of the behavior of bears confronting the explorers matched other meticulous descriptions of distances, compass bearings, river conditions, plants, and animals. From this I concluded that their accounts of contacts with grizzly bears were unadorned with embellishments, as did Theodore Roosevelt, when he commented that Lewis and Clark "have drawn their descriptions with such complete freedom from exaggeration."

Grizzly Bears: Not a Problem

To analyze the interactions with grizzlies, I transcribed every description of bear-human interactions in all eleven volumes of Gary Moulton's *The Definitive Journals of Lewis and Clark* (2001). Grizzly bear entries are indexed under the headings: "hunted," "observed," and "attacked by," for a total of 132 entries. Fifty-five descriptions were sufficiently complete to determine who initiated an approach, who made the first aggressive move, and whether a bear or a person was wounded or killed. (Their descriptions were so similar to my field notes on bear-human interactions around Brooks Camp that I could do a similar analysis.)

Folklore and serious literature in books and essays on the Lewis and Clark expedition create the impression that the expedition's crew had constant trouble with grizzly bears along the Missouri River and across the Rockies. For example, in his book, *Our Natural History: The Lessons of Lewis and Clark*, Daniel Botkin describes grizzlies as "vicious, the most especially troublesome," adding that "encounters with grizzly bears were their most dangerous encounters with any animal and among the most dangerous of all their experiences" (p. 86). Moulton, a recognized scholar and editor of the journals, leaves a similarly misleading impression. The major index entry for grizzlies pretty much says it all: "Bears, grizzly, attacks by." This suggests that the entries about grizzly bears could all be seen as attacks, but my research did not turn up any examples. My line-by-line analysis of Lewis and Clark's encounters with grizzlies revealed that expedition members, not grizzlies, were the aggressors. Grizzlies, not humans, were the only ones injured or killed. During the entire expedition, hunting parties shot and killed fifty-one grizzly bears, with an additional eighteen grizzlies wounded.

So pervasive is the prejudice toward the "horrible" bear that encounters are almost invariably interpreted as attacks. How could grizzly bears get so much bad press if no one had been injured, let alone killed, by a bear despite all their contacts? Powerful and fearsome they are but not vicious and primed to attack at every encounter. That's what the journals say. It's even more astonishing to find that after 210 years, no authors appear to have gleaned the actual facts from these wonderfully accurate accounts.

Here is an excerpt of Lewis's description of a grizzly bear approach, which has been widely interpreted as an attack.

> 12 June 1805
>
> . . . and having entirely forgotten to reload my rifle, a large white bear, or rather brown bear, had perceived and crept up on me within 20 steps before I discovered him; in the first moment I drew up my gun to shoot, but at the same instance recollected that she was not loaded . . .. he was then briskly advancing on me . . .. in this situation I thought of retreating in a brisk walk as fast as he was advancing . . .. I had no sooner turned myself about but he pitched at me, open mouthed and full speed, I ran about 80 yards and found he gained on me fast, I then run into the water . . .. I ran hastily into the water about waist deep, and faced about . . .. at this instance he arrived at the edge of the water within about 20 feet of me; the moment I put myself in this attitude of defense he suddenly wheeled about . . .. and retreated with quite as great precipitation as he had just before pursued me.

My experience with Alaskan bears tells me this was an approach by a curious bear, perhaps to see if there was a meal to be had. As Lewis hurried away, the bear responded with a quicker pace. Hikers, take note! But when Lewis turned and confronted the grizzly with his spear, it reverted to escape behavior, another response that I have used with a can of pepper spray—rarely necessary with Brooks River bears. Lewis writes that the bear ran at him "full speed" but did not catch him after eighty yards, certainly an exaggeration. Let's dispense with the "full speed" description, as grizzlies can outrun a racehorse in a short spurt. Was poor old Lewis letting his fear interfere with his recall?

We all recognize that large, powerful animals, such as killer whales, are capable of carnage with their teeth. The same is true with grizzlies. But we cannot equate that fact with a certainty of a vicious attack whenever contact with people is made. In the case of the Lewis and Clark expedition, the majority of first contacts (forty-eight) between grizzlies and the party were hunting approaches by the men, compared to five approaches by bears. Who was the aggressor? The hunting parties overwhelmingly initiated contact. Case closed!

This explanation is simple but inconvenient to those who want grizzlies to remain horrible: the boatmen went out to hunt and kill grizzly bears for *food*. If the grizzlies were so aggressive and ferocious, one would expect to read about a few injuries from the bears. There were none. The journals clearly state that grizzlies attempted to escape from hunting parties whenever they could. When the hunters were chased or "attacked" by grizzlies, it was mostly in response to shooting and wounding. In the most commonly cited "attack," quoted above, Lewis escaped into a river. The bear's slow approach suggests curiosity, since the distances covered and elapsed times are too long for this to be an attack. Insisting that grizzlies are dangerous goes against the facts. Dangerous when wounded? No doubt. The ballistic force of their rifle balls, despite being propelled by the best-available French gunpowder, was feeble compared to modern rifles. Another contribution to danger involved with their muzzle-loading rifles was that they required over thirty seconds to reload. They needed up to six people shooting to stop a charging bear before it got to them. This explains why the expedition assembled so many hunters to kill a grizzly.

Grizzlies were pursued despite the risks, because the expedition wanted their fat to add to their larder. Bear fat made lean deer, elk, and pronghorn antelope meat palatable. Rowing, poling, and hauling loaded boats upstream all day demanded a prodigious amount of energy.

Animal fat has the highest caloric density of any food. One large bear carcass provided eight gallons of rendered fat. This explains why sighting a grizzly on an opposite bank caused encamped hunters to jump into a boat and row over to kill it.

The continuous negative stereotyping of grizzlies is perhaps the most profound message that comes from the misinterpretation of Lewis and Clark's journals. Scholars have repeated the popular myths rather than decipher the written accounts. Small wonder we suffer from a bad attitude toward these animals and treat them as hostile creatures to target.

Tolerance for the "Evil Bear"

Demonizing grizzly bears goes back to first contacts. Settlers, cattle ranchers, and sheepherders trapped, poisoned, and shot them, almost causing their extinction. A savvy adversary, the grizzly frequently avoided traps and outwitted trappers to continue killing livestock. Old Ephraim of Utah folklore had a reputation for cunning and was said to remove massive leg-hold traps set for him. It took trapper Frank Clark over 9 years before he finally caught and killed the old veteran in 1923, but not before the bear had killed about 150 sheep. Ernest Thompson Seton says it well in his 1937 *Lives of Game Animals.*

> Each year the number of hunters increases; each year more deadly traps, subtler poisons and more irresistible guns are out to get the Grizzly. He has no chance at all of escape. There is no closed season, no new invulnerability to meet the new perils. He is absolutely at the mercy of those who know no mercy. And before five years more, I expect to learn that there are no Grizzlies left in the United States, except in the Yellowstone Park, that last blessed haven of the fugitive from inevitable and nearly universal destruction.

Hatred toward grizzlies runs deep even among those who had never seen a grizzly bear. While attitudes are changing about sharks, gorillas, and killer whales, grizzlies still carry the stigma of timeworn folklore: an unpredictable rogue, always ready to charge and dismember a person. To be sure, grizzlies are fast, powerful predators and rarely grant pardon if surprised at close range—never mind that dogs can behave the same way. Consider that the ratio of the size of a big dog to a child is similar to that of a grizzly to an adult human. When a dog bites an adult, it is rarely news, but a grizzly mauling is *always* news, similar to when a dog mauls a child.

My favorite bear bigots are those who find malevolent intent in grizzlies, as embodied in the expression "they kill for pleasure," a combination of fear and prejudice toward the bear. As an explanation, the phrase has no meaning. Killing is what predators do. Yes, escaping prey can trigger a wired-in capture-kill response, like your cat chasing a string. If you conclude that a raccoon in a chicken coop kills all the chickens because it can, then adding that it does so for pleasure offers nothing except moral indignation or a sense of superiority. When a grizzly kills dozens of sheep, does the expression fit better, bordering on psychopathology?

Specialists in predator behavior label this phenomenon "surplus killing," defined as any situation where carnivores kill more prey than they can eat at one time. Without digressing into the weeds of evolutionary explanations, consider that wolves, hyenas, bears, and other predators may, on occasion, be faced with prey whose defense mechanisms are blunted from domestication or unusual circumstances. Domestic sheep come close to being thoroughly defenseless, totally dependent on herder protection.

Renowned field ecologist Hans Kruuk explained surplus killing well as a type of accident or misfiring of normal behavioral sequences. Early one morning on the Serengeti Plains of East Africa, Kruuk came upon dozens of severely injured antelopes and a few carcasses that had been fed on. He discovered the mayhem after a night made totally dark by a severe prolonged rainstorm, with rolling thunder and lightning. Hyenas had attacked a resting herd of antelope. Kruuk surmised that the antelope had been unaware of the predators' approach and had no effective or adaptive response to escape the hyenas. Demonizing the hyenas for killing "for pleasure" in that situation made no more sense than it does for grizzly bears.

Toward A More Honest View of Grizzly Bears

After recovering from my grizzly bear encounter, I resumed my research on bear behavior in Alaska, a welcome career change. In 1983, Katmai National Park was casting around for a qualified person who might bring some science to park concerns about potential risks to humans and the brown bears of Brooks River. At the time, I was scribbling some thoughts about bear adaptation to people and realized this was an opportunity to test some of my hypotheses.

Katmai's bear manager, Kathy Jope, had designed a study inspired by her grizzly bear experiences in Montana's Glacier National Park. She liked my proposal and facilitated the funding for a study. The study at Brooks River turned my university career around and helped prepare three students for jobs in bear management.

At Brooks Camp, my confidence grew, even though I was amongst the densest population of brown bears in North America. Coming to Alaska, with a river and a waterfall alive with thousands of salmon, was not just an opportunity and a fabulous gift. The growing popularity of Brooks Camp and the political decisions by Alaska's senators to refuse limits on visitor numbers made for a fascinating agenda, both biologically and politically. It involved numerous challenges for research in a site that was as close to its prehistoric makeup as one could imagine.

After surviving my devastating accident in Yellowstone, I wanted to champion grizzlies. My commitment to maintain the wild in national parks was deep. I was at home in the outdoors, seeing large, wild mammals as they were seen in Paleolithic times. Doing field science with enthusiastic students buttressed my enduring optimism that rationality could overcome mythology and the greed and ignorance that threatens natural systems. In many ways, grizzly bears cluster with wolves, dolphins, apes, and elephants as cultures, highly social civilizations that we barely understand. We treat them as consumable resources instead of recognizing them as challenges to our humanity and degree of civility. Henry Beston best expressed this sentiment.

> We patronize them for their incompleteness, for their tragic fate of having taken form so far below ourselves. And therein we err, and greatly err. For the animal shall not be measured by man. In a world older and more complete than ours they move finished and complete, gifted with extensions of the senses we have lost or never attained, living by voices we shall never hear. They are not brethren, they are not underlings; they are other nations, caught with ourselves in the net of life and time, fellow prisoners of the splendor and travail of the earth.

Working Wilderness in Katmai National Park

It was not too late to preserve the essential linkage of salmon to bears in this wild, protected landscape. To recognize the significance of the Pacific salmon's contribution to the integrity of wild ecosystems is to appreciate the key role grizzlies play.

In the summer of 1991, I was captivated by the consequences of bears moving parts of salmon upslope to distant watersheds, depositing fertilizer along with berry seeds over their spellbinding network of trails.

If bears had that major function, then the old view that they would just be replaced by another process in the food chain was obsolete. To me this was a powerful role to understand and add to the worth of grizzly bears.

Factoring in geological time scales to the transporting process implies an enormous scattering of seeds and fertilizer by bears and a hundred other species. The neo-environmentalists who spout a "new and better" ideology of humankind's gardening in the Anthropocene have not grasped the true nature of a "working landscape," a wilderness factory with fish, plants, and animals pumping out productivity in a manner that would warm the heart of Henry Ford.

At Brooks River, bears streamed in, including females with cubs, quickly learning the tricks of preying on big fish. The wariest bears fed at night or early in the morning before people appeared, or so we thought. Over time the impressively large, dominant males became more abundant, according to the detailed records of Tamara Olson, who the park service was lucky to engage as chief bear biologist after her thesis project. The bear growth numbers concentrating on record numbers of sockeye salmon posed some intriguing questions. What if the effect of all the discarded fish parts, scavengers' urine, and feces was interrupted? And what about any loss of the bodies of all the critters eating salmon and eventually dying in the forests, fertilizing the landscape's vegetation? I advocated the long-term view: the annual migrations of salmon upstream and upslope into lakes and streams replenishes nutrients lost as water carries nitrates and phosphates down to the ocean, a nutrient sink. We quipped that the salmon were "care packages" sent by Mother Ocean to her upslope terrestrial children. If one watched how happy bears were to catch a salmon, one saw the humor.

To circle back to the public's negative typecasting of bears, people may think me daft to portray grizzlies as harmless or benign. All bears—white, black, and brown—prey on people on occasion, often leading to the most frightening, gory, heart-rending outcomes. Am I explaining away their predatory nature? Not really. Statistically, grizzlies are more dangerous than cougars or wolves. Our safety depends on how appropriately we respond while developing an ethic of respect, not stereotyping them as villains to target with hatred and destruction.

The huge Alaskan brown bears of Brooks River may be the most benign bears living among people anywhere on Earth. Even the most cautious of us cannot help but acquire an attitude change about grizzly bears after an afternoon at Brooks. Mine came surprising quickly while walking and working among them. The outcome from my Alaskan conversion was a deep skepticism about all the horror stories about grizzlies, and later, a growing curiosity about the basic character of "natural" grizzlies, those bears that have not been trapped, darted, sedated, collared, or shot at. Not an easy order to serve up, but some trails to truth exist to be followed. The expedition journals of William Clark and Meriwether Lewis are a good place to start. They tell us that grizzlies and people are compatible—as long as humans behave themselves.

4

Bears as Friends

One sunny summer afternoon in 1987, a massive male bear showed astonishing tolerance toward me as it rested in the woods near Brooks River. Thoughtlessly, I was rushing off trail through some trees toward the lake shore. (Impatience is never a good idea in Old Ephraim country: better to aim your radar far into the woods.) As I neared the shore, the 700–800-pounder sprang off the ground and trundled away. Another ten feet, and I would have stepped right on him. The bear gave me a startled stare, as if to say, "I thought we had an agreement that you would stay on your trails and leave the woods to us." He might just as easily have bluff-charged me. That, or worse, would not be uncommon in grizzly country elsewhere. My guess is that these big, old regulars have suffered a hundred thoughtless indignities from people over a lifetime. He was not threatened. Most bears at Brooks focus on eating, sleeping, and avoiding other bears. People are treated like annoying magpies, neither threatening nor feeding the bears. The same is true with many animals, in that respectful people are pretty much ignored, and habituation reigns. Bears also ignore other bears, when appropriate.

Observing bears in autumn at Brooks adds excitement because of the surge in bear numbers, and many bear-to-bear contacts means opportunities to watch interactions. Dead and dying salmon are everywhere. Defending turf makes no sense. Bears want to eat, not fight. Here is an example of how they avoid spats.

In 1999, we stayed into mid-October, after guests and staff had departed Brooks River Camp. Facilities were boarded up for the winter, leaving bears happily targeting fish carcasses accumulating on the lower river. I chose a cabin roof for a panoramic view overlooking the marsh and estuary. Right away I scoped a distant sub-adult bear searching for carcasses below a six-foot-high cut bank. Suddenly, right above him, a huge male poked his massive head out of the tall grass and scanned across the stream. The smaller bear froze, knowing he was way too close. At first the big guy showed no discernible reaction. Then he slowly swung his head off to the side, as if to say, "I'm cutting you some slack here, so clear out." The youngster remained transfixed. The big bank bear repeated his gesture with an exaggerated head swing to the side. The subordinate bear took this cue and scooted off. The entire routine looked rehearsed, but it was probably some kind of communication ritual, not unlike our face-saving tricks.

Careful attention to bear signaling offers a primer in bear language and as well as safety tips for people who may blunder too close to a grizzly. Usually, bears take time to assess a situation. We should too. A large, locally dominant bear has little to gain by threatening or challenging a smaller bear, and he risks getting a return bite in a brawl. His biological imperative is to put on weight for a long stint in a winter den. By swinging his head sideways, the bear has declared little interest; a direct stare might signal an impending attack. When his eyes were averted, the smaller bear could escape without triggering a bite in the butt. The same is true with people near a grizzly. The rule is always: do not run. If you run, you may trigger an attack by communicating that you are subordinate, even suggesting that you could be on the menu. In addition, when you run, your vulnerable parts are exposed, and your weapons, if any, are facing away. Far better to keep the dominant guy guessing, even by bluffing. Bears are unsure of the risks we pose, and if no carcass or other food is being defended, bears will usually avoid the risk of getting hurt and move on. This seems to apply widely—but not always—in bear-bear and people-bear interactions.

Reflecting on my own bear encounter, you might wonder why I ran when a grizzly charged me. Quite a different situation. When I faced my special nightmare, she was already charging me. I had moved quickly over a spur ridge right into her lap. I wasn't paying attention, assuming oh so incorrectly, that being atop a nine-thousand-foot mountain would put me above all the bears I had seen below. I panicked upon seeing a big angry grizzly charging right at me and turned to escape. To stand and face her (with no bear spray—not yet invented—and no weapon) was not a defensive mode. I had failed the awareness test and blundered way inside her personal space.

The bear on the bank story is a calmer tale that shows how grizzlies can delay responses. I have watched hundreds of such responses to fishermen wading in Brooks River as well as other places. Early in our research, we concluded, confidently but incorrectly, that the bears were tolerant, because they stayed rather than avoiding immediately. Later review of our data sheets told a different story. We discovered that after five to ten minutes, bears moved slowly to a stream bank and disappeared into the forest. The long delay between cause and effect muddied any clear interpretation about disturbances by people, one of our primary research objectives. Immediate avoidance or fast retreat was not a common way for bears to react. Delaying retreat might be a bear's way of avoiding a show of subordinate status, even if fearful of attack. It fits with a pattern in mammals that attempt to avoid a series of losses in dominance-subordinate disputes. Like people, bears can learn to be losers in interactions, which they attempt to avoid.

Salmon bears can pose serious risks of injury to people, especially in the spring if a hungry bear has commandeered a moose carcass or a mother with cubs is surprised at close quarters. Again, generalizing about threats from bears is complex: context is everything! Timothy Treadwell's sad death (made famous in Werner Herzog's documentary *Grizzly Man*) from a coastal Katmai predatory bear taught us that not all bears react to people by benignly adapting to our presence. Tim went thirteen years without a serious mishap among tolerant bears, despite his video footage showing that he often harassed them by approaching too close.

Tim first telephoned me in December 1993, when he told me about his filming plans.

"Barrie, the bears are bumping into my tent at night," he said.

"Tim," I replied, "if a bear bumps your tent, it's not an accident. You should get away from the bear trails where you're camping. They aren't happy."

His camp was deep in thick alders and birch where bear trails converged. He sloughed off my suggestion to use elevated platforms and electric fences. He continued pressing bears and filming them for years—until his luck ran out. On the night of October 5, 2003, Tim and his partner, Amy Huguenard, were killed in their camp by an old, thin male with bad teeth, according to official reports.

The Elusive Grizzly

Almost tripping over a napping big bear and emerging unscathed might seem like a lucky break. But for a bear near a salmon stream with mobs of people and bears, stalemate is a good plan. When bears have plenty of grub and learn not to break people's stuff, they are treated as guests.

In Katmai and Brooks River, bears come first (except in camp—more on this later). Other grizzlies in North America have no such tolerance for people at close range, giving biologists with grizzly contacts a dramatically different perception.

This difference in experience came to me when outside experts visited Brooks Camp. They perceived high risks to tourists from Brooks bears. The two grizzly bear biologists, Chris Servheen and John Schoen, made a quick survey at the invitation of the NPS and reported back. Their memo to the Alaskan regional director contained an astonishing conclusion. It stated that Brooks Camp was the "most dangerous bear-human interaction situation" that they knew of and that "the issue is not if a death or injury will occur, it is when it will happen." They were not persuaded by forty years of management without a significant injury, nor did their report cite a decade of behavioral study by park biologist Tamara Olson and my other students' reports. Although the two experts provided some useful management suggestions, they seem to have misunderstood or discounted the differences between the extreme habituation of bears to people on salmon streams like Brooks River and the extreme avoidance, in general, by grizzlies in mountain parks in the lower forty-eight, such as Yellowstone and Glacier national parks. Bears adjusting to many other bears, feeding on salmon, is a parallel situation to their adjusting to anglers, aircraft pilots, and aggressive photographers sharing the river with them. This fits with the rule that when surplus food is available, better to feed than fight. Sometimes embedded assumptions trump facts.

On the other hand, the number of bears at Brooks has increased substantially, as have the number of visitors. If salmon numbers crash in the future, those outside consultants may prove to be right with their call for caution. And there is always the Treadwell bear to consider, similar to a large male bear that visitors watched in horror as it ate the back out of a younger bear in mid-stream. A park ranger was summoned to escort the terrified people back to camp. So much for friendly habituated bears.

In 1983, when I began research on bear behavior for the NPS in Katmai Park, I carried unknown mental baggage about risks from grizzlies. I had the strongest possible reason to be wary of grizzlies, brandishing lifelong scars from a near-death experience by a Yellowstone grizzly in 1977. Enthusiasm helped overcome my initial anxiety during my first weeks in Brooks Camp. By late summer, I was walking alone at night back to my tent through woods so dark that I had to feel with my feet for the trail. I had been escorting nervous visitors back to their cabins from the lodge in inky darkness and then had to get home without a flashlight. This marked an emotional plateau in overcoming residual fear from my thrashing six years earlier. Oddly, I never experienced bear nightmares, still a mystery to me. Could it be that I had told the grisly story so many times that there was no script left for bad dreams?

In 1990, I recognized a new brand of bear at Brooks Camp at season's end, one that steered clear of people and could be very dangerous. They appeared after the lodge and facilities were closed and winterized. Their cue that humans had gone was the silence replacing the racket from ATVs and diesel generators. Time to reclaim the river. Because our research team stayed after the camp went quiet, these bears may have been confused and even upset. For our safety, we modified our daily protocols to increase vigilance. We would only hike in pairs to observation platforms and, most importantly, we disposed of our assumptions about "nice bears" that our summer experiences had encouraged. Seeing a new bear on a trail ahead meant giving way sooner than the suggested fifty yards, even leaving the area, unless the bear telegraphed no apparent problem with our presence.

So, my bear world has the usual diverse characters and a few villains. To conclude that some bears hate people may invite shaming for anthropomorphism, but a bear's behavior can be shaped by extreme hunger, painful experiences with people, and the evolutionary imperatives driving infanticide among large males. Contending with grizzlies safely at close range requires a game plan, starting with gauging the bear's motivation or intentions. For those of us addicted to observing unknown grizzlies, an appropriate back-up defense is completely rational for that small but finite opportunity for catastrophe. In Timothy Treadwell's worldview, personal defense was off the table. I settled on a combination of bear spray and shotguns for work in wild country, especially when I was mentoring new students, who were beginning work on unfamiliar turf. My mind lingered on that outstanding killer, living outside the box of normal bears. I hardened my empathic heart for bears and swore to never lose any more tissue to any bear. On the other hand, wild country with grizzlies comes with risks. I can accept that. It is part of the wilderness that we love, as my deep-ethics friend, Doug Peacock, and others have helped us understand.

5

Coming Home: The Real Bear

A Passion for Place: Dealing with Demons

The pilot throttled back the floatplane's engine to glide us quietly down to the burnished surface of Naknek Lake. In the distance was the sandy pumice beach of Brooks Camp. I had just flown high over Alaska's rugged coastal range on my way to Katmai National Park to launch a grizzly bear study. Although new to Alaska, I felt strangely like I was coming home. The cold rivers and lakes with infinite vistas sparked fond memories of a childhood spent exploring the wave-lashed shores of Lake Ontario. Only one mismatch: this place was swarming with giant bears, and I was too few years from surviving a savage mauling by a Yellowstone Park grizzly. Yes, this study was my choice. I had submitted a proposal for research on bear behavior and safety concerns for park visitors. Had I arrived in Alaska to put some suppressed fears to the test? As the park superintendent helped me down from the aircraft floats to shore, I was about to find out. A large furry animal was making its way toward us from down the beach.

In Alaska my passion for wild was re-ignited. Each trip into Katmai revealed new wonders. Katmai's beaches, lined with stunted spruce and alder, painted an inviting portrait of nature. Its historic log cabins and dirt paths offered a slice of nature to feed the spirit. Stepping off a plane was stepping into the past. The primitive fishing camp cast a romantic aura of a simpler time, reaching back further into prehistory, when only massive bears dominated that wilderness setting. Where could one find nature like this in our ever-diminishing spaces and crowded places? A hike to Brooks Falls was the cure—an encounter with a bear on its turf and on its terms. Magical.

My inaugural arrival in 1984, fresh from bear work in Yellowstone and Yosemite, churned up personal baggage from those experiences, not least of all bureaucratic politics. When I stepped off the float plane into Brooks Camp, I bore a face disfigured by a Yellowstone grizzly but no ill will toward bears or park managers, for that matter. Although I was new to Alaska, I was not treated like an outsider (not then at least). At the start, I was wary of being tagged as the "bear expert," a trap for a new guy among experienced rangers. Right off the bat, a ranger asked what I thought was needed to manage the bears and people more safely. Taking that bait would have jeopardized the future credibility of our project.

I settled into the dark, cold wall tent that had been assigned to me: a site at the end of staff housing but too embedded in trees for my growing unease about big bears. Nevertheless, it was immensely enjoyable, like an exotic camping trip into semi-wild country. But that first night, I lay wide awake in my down sleeping bag in the upper tent's loft, visualizing how easily a bear could claw through the tent and drag me out. What flash of insanity landed me there? Within two days, however, in the company of a very competent ranger, Kathy Jope, I settled into a routine. The project put my university career back on track and heralded forty years of fascinating up-close study of wild grizzly bears. Little did I realize what unique access I would have to the minds of these complex beings.

I watched one mom searching for fish mid-river while her spring cub struggled to keep abreast of her on shore. Frustrated, the cub waded into the swift water and swam to its mother. Sahale, a lovely name that my student, Anne Braaten gave her, vented her displeasure at the grasping cub by lashing out with a paw, slapping the cub below the surface. The cub popped up and returned to shore, pronto. Thoughtlessly, I condemned this brutal move, and then I recognized her wisdom. If she did not get fish, her cubs would not get milk. Good as a mother bear can be, if a cub failed to wait on shore, punishment shaped behavior. The cub got the message.

Mother bears face the dilemma of keeping young nearby for safety but loosening that bond to go into dangerously fast water, where fish can be caught. This illustrates the intelligence bears display, a kind of tough love, bear style.

Another delightful story about how bears think circulated around Brooks Camp. A young woman was making her way alone along the forest trail to the viewing platform overlooking Brooks Falls. Ahead in the lovely open forest she saw a big bear—well, maybe not so big, but to me they all looked big when alone in the woods. It approached her slowly, probably full of salmon and on its way to a daybed to rest and digest. As the woman's anxiety grew, she dimly remembered some advice about playing dead. So, she dropped down, curled up, and kept still. Soon another person happened along, saw the situation, and ran back to get help from a ranger at the trailhead, minutes away. As the ranger approached, he saw the alarmed lady on the ground, then noticed nearby, a sleeping bear. Only one explanation seems to work here. This bear was accustomed to people and reacted to the person reclining as it would to a friendly companion bear: "You think this is a safe place to snooze, I'll join you because I'm groggy and full of fish." Bears have the ability to recognize that there is strength in numbers: two can share vigilance if trouble threatens.

This bear was not interested in playing dominance games of displacing or charging anybody. This story shows that bears are more willing to think of humans as a bear than vice versa. It strengthens what experienced naturalists like Charlie Russell told us, that our fear of bears is unrealistic. Most of the time, they not only don't want to hurt us, they even watch us and take cues about how secure a situation may be for them. We can live in harmony with bears if we choose, but not if we are hung up about being eaten—sometimes being completely overwhelmed by the idea that this animal is extremely dangerous, even though it isn't. Could this be part of why native people admired and learned from bears but also had great respect for bears' prodigious strength? Using my background and experience in ethology, I was discovering what a scientist in mid-life might contribute.

In the late 1980s, on the same trail from Brooks Falls, I met Conan, the biggest adult male on the river. He walked directly toward us as I guided Utah Senator Wayne Owens and his three companions. A group of five was a bonus for meeting any bear. This lumbering behemoth filled the trail—so massive one might be excused for thinking it was an elephant covered by a fur rug. The forest nearby had sparse understory plants, so we could head off trail anywhere. I immediately assumed the role of the calm expert, a good option even when alone. On the down side, I was the guy who had survived a mauling, hoping no flashback of that terror would erupt. By cajoling myself into a state of self-assurance, I adopted the leadership role to guide my companions out of danger and told everyone to follow me off the trail. I had no problem giving a powerful politician advice when an eight-hundred-pound bear was fast approaching.

The big bear carried on down the trail. I was feeling smug in the role of bear guru, right up to the moment when Conan turned toward us and now stood forty to fifty yards from us. Holy crap! Now he really had my attention. Flashing through my mind was a new relationship—the predator-prey relationship. When a carnivore keeps orienting toward you, it is not looking for a companion but showing a flesh-eating interest in you. However, as soon as we stepped aside a second time, the bear kept going without as much as a glance toward us. Just by coincidence, I had led my group in the direction that Conan used to go to his daybed. Another instance of reciprocal tolerance where grizzly bears are protected and well fed.

These interactions resonate with my central theme, that we can live in harmony with bears, if we choose. They tell a story that our fear of bears is unrealistic. They don't want to hurt us; in fact, they even take some of their cues and good ideas from us, if we let them. As the late naturalist Charlie Russell was fond of saying, we rarely listen to bears to hear what they are saying.

The Anthropological Bear

My initial contact with the new science of ethology (the study of the behavior of free-living animals) was in the 1960s as a graduate student working under Dr. Peter Klopfer, a brilliant young addition to the Department of Zoology at Duke University. One of few essential books that Peter suggested I read was Frank Fraser Darling's *A Herd of Red Deer,* which embodied all the subtle field techniques to observe the social life of wild animals. Darling's observational approach was emulated by George Schaller with gorillas and later by Jane Goodall in her chimpanzee research at Gombe in 1960. She joined Louis Leakey, without any training, to study apes, an initiative to gain insight into human origins. I met Dr. Leakey at Duke to interview for possible work in Africa, not realizing he always chose women to study apes. The opportunity came to naught when I admitted I had no outside funding.

Shortly after that, I jumped at another opportunity that Peter arranged. He had recommended me as a research assistant to study bottle-nosed dolphins in the Virgin Islands, working with renowned anthropologist Gregory Bateson. If dream jobs drop from heaven, this was one for me. One drawback prevented any semblance of naturalistic studies: the three dolphins were confined to a small pool in a laboratory that Dr. John Lilly had constructed for inter-species communication research. Bateson, however, had a disciplined observational approach to pursuing non-verbal communication in whales and octopus. I had completed a master's degree and hoped to find a question for doctoral research on animal behavior while assisting his work. We learned how bright dolphins were, but I failed to find how observing three captive dolphins might present questions for further graduate work. After a short sojourn in Hawaii doing more dolphin social studies, I returned to Duke to continue research on imprinting in newborn deer using the methods of quantitative ethology.

I have doubled back to my scientific background, so you can see how this type of behavioral study of bears might contribute to better management of bears at Brooks River. Experience with social animals like deer, dolphins, and pronghorn gave me some confidence that observing grizzlies interacting with people on a salmon stream in a national park would provide useful information on the different responses of bears to visitors. For example, are mothers with cubs especially sensitive to disturbances? Do older males become tolerant of people after years of contact with anglers and photographers? Is there a special problem with an aggressive approach for food by sub-adult bears that are both hungrier and lower on the dominance scale than older bears? These and other questions, important to managing people and improving safety around bears, could be answered by identifying individuals. Concentrating observations would help accumulate enough data to see trends and establish generalities.

In 1967, one of the earliest calls for management-oriented research at Brooks Camp was in Dr. Frederick Dean's report on his bear-human study, which sensitized me to the park's delaying tactics, which continue to this day. Next came Will Troyer's study responding to the

1974 superintendent's request for "information gathered with as little harassment of bears as possible," although capturing and collaring was acceptable, it seems. By 1986 the general management plan repeated the objective to relocate all or parts of Brooks Camp, as Dean and Troyer recommended. Regrettably, after thirty years of consistently finding that Brooks Camp is in the wrong place, decisions are still guided by financial interests and their elected servants rather than by the long-term conservation values that the law mandates. (I explore this issue further in part three of this book.

To address potential impacts of humans on Brooks bears' behavior, in 1984, I introduced a novel approach to quantifying sampling that captured the amount of time that bears and people were observed in three zones on the lower river. I did this to ensure that later studies could compare a future study with ours using a rigorous quantifying method. This approach described bear activity in terms of bear hours for every hour of observation. For example, following four bears over a one-hour period gave an activity rate of four bear hours per observation hour. By sampling evenly in all three observation zones through each weekly cycle, we could analyze time budgets for bears when different levels of human use were tallied. If another study began many years later, a biologist could repeat our methodology from the same locations and determine what changes, if any, had occurred in the bears' use of the river. This protocol for study has similarities with other animal behavior studies and perhaps cultural anthropology (ethnology). Our goals were more oriented to specific effects on bears or people and less on a complete ethogram (i.e., a depiction of all aspects of an animal's behavior).

After my student, Tamara Olson, completed her MS thesis, she returned to Katmai as a wildlife biologist and continued to apply her formidable enthusiasm for systematic sampling of bear behavior. She compiled nine years of data and reports. This work showed in great detail the negative effects on some bears of occupation of the bears' habitat at all hours of the day and some at night. Despite an anti-science attitude by advocates for the lodge and other businesses regarding findings that might restrain their activities, park superintendent G. Ray Bane saw the value and implications of this research and acted to reduce impacts in accordance with the park's management plan and federal legal mandates. He was opposed at many levels, including lodge employees, fishing guides, and aircraft pilots, who never read the research reports or came up with contrary findings. They chose to promote a variety of values and management plans that were far from sustainable compared to bear-viewing operations at other locations in the USA and Canada. The ensuing fiasco has been reported elsewhere but not here, because it is too complicated. Despite the restrictions placed on the NPS by Alaskan senators to use our research, the techniques employed provided the kind of refined results regarding impacts on bears that were required.

Still, the challenge and opportunity to apply these less-intrusive studies on grizzlies in other locations is valid. In the Yellowstone ecosystem, the tradition of capturing grizzlies with traps and darts and collaring them has carried on for fifty years. This could be justified at the beginning of population recovery in the 1970s, but handling bears is no longer necessary with other less-intrusive techniques, such as examining hair and scats, DNA techniques, and trail cameras, which permit one to identify almost all the bears in an area by direct observation. It would also be useful to have detailed observations of uncaptured free-ranging bears, if only to compare the effects of capture on individual animals. There is sufficient awareness of aggressiveness in handled bears to warrant a study to answer questions about the impacts of this intrusion.

Another reason for ending bear handling can be appreciated from studies of mountain gorillas and chimpanzees. None of the studies of these great apes has required capture and collaring to obtain detailed life history, habitat use, and behavior information, despite their threatened status. Apes and bears need more habitat and less wanton destruction of their habitat by people. If the effort to count animals was transferred to action to expand habitat and security for grizzlies, then the growth of bear populations would be known from expansion into former range and wilderness areas. The application of ethological techniques would offer the means to measure success in multiple ways. Our work in Katmai was a start.

Like many field biologists, I received my science training steeped in objective facts only—little room for anthropomorphism in interpreting bear behavior. Keeping track of bears with quirky personalities called for a more liberal approach. Why does interpretation of bear behavior need to be so restrictive? Disciplined anthropomorphism should be encouraged, so empathy can open doors to the mental lives of animals.

My extensive observations of Brooks bears revealed novel cultural patterns—startling behavioral innovations passed on to other bears. Grizzlies deserve to be classed with other big-brained mammals that transmit learned behavior socially. For example, I discovered that Brooks bears were specializing their feeding on a single run of salmon over the entire Brooks River watershed. As I described earlier, the bears first target fish leaping Brooks Falls, then follow trails to shallow streams to catch nest-building salmon. Finally, the bears turn back to Brooks to gorge on dying salmon drifting into Naknek Lake. This four-month odyssey of bears tracking tens of thousands of salmon requires a closer look before its uniqueness is lost. The onslaught of anglers and the monetizing of a bear sideshow is degrading Brooks River with industrial-strength tourism. So far, national laws, park bureaucracy, and major environmental organizations have failed to defend the wonders and magic of Katmai. Only courage to confront short-term financial greed can preserve the natural and archeological resources of the Brooks River area.

The beauty of wild nature, an awareness of how much more is here than the material world, has filtered in through the astonishing diversity of the behavior of these super-sentient bears and later by the complexity of the bears' role in cycling material and transferring energy over millennia. This revered heritage is highlighted by the contrast between Brooks

River's wild and the engineered world of sprawling Anchorage outside my airplane window. The quintessential rarity of Brooks dazzles as a truly wild watershed. This vast landscape, defined by salmon homing up sparkling rivers to spawn and die, has nourished the land and creatures since the continental glaciers faded away. It also nourishes our spirit.

6

Why Bears Attack

Defensive Tactics by Females with Cubs

Not all grizzlies conform to the pattern of habituated Brooks bears. Overall, grizzlies account for more attacks than cougars and wolves, by far. So, some balance is needed to avoid unfortunate generalizations. In the first chapter, I related how the female grizzly that ran me down was likely the one we had watched earlier with three cubs confronting a big male. If so, she would have walked about a half mile through forest, climbing to her daybed retreat, where I disturbed her.

We saw no cubs in our brief encounter on the ridge, but they could have been over the edge out of sight.

A number of factors may have fed her aggressive behavior. Right after the rescue, a park biologist found a grizzly daybed nearby with fresh scats around it, suggesting a bear returned there regularly. Choosing a high alpine site without food around may have been her strategy to avoid grizzly traffic while resting. A surprise invasion of her space could account for her intense defensive response.

Earlier in the day, we had seen her avoid a big male. In a defensive/aggressive mood, she may have been primed that morning to hit almost anything bothering her. Wherever I have studied black bears and grizzly bears—in the Rockies, coastal British Columbia (BC), and Alaska—they seek out places secure from intrusion, where they can rest and digest their meals. Many of these daybeds overlook bear trails or are in heavy cover. On the forested slopes of coastal BC, daybeds are commonly located snug up to the trunks of large cedar trees, maybe to guard their backs. In my attack, I accidently invaded her inner sanctum. She charged to counter the threat. Stephen Herrero has documented and explained many similar attacks in his widely acclaimed book, *Bear Attacks: Their Cause and Avoidance.*

I believe there could be another reason for a fight-to-the-death strategy in grizzlies. If a threat is detected at some distance by a mother with young cubs, she may be hard-pressed to keep them together. Accounts are not uncommon of attacks launched by females from three hundred or more yards, leaving their cubs behind. I suspect there is a genetic predisposition for this tactic, a behavior unknown in black bears. Grizzlies probably evolved in treeless areas, either alpine, prairie or tundra habitat. Although other locations may be forested, like feeding sites near streams or in wet meadows, few trees are nearby for cub protection. Unlike their parents, grizzly cubs have claws suited to climbing, useful for eluding a charging male, which requires quick action and a high perch. But on open ground, a mother's protective actions might be explained by the challenge of staying near multiple cubs. If she follows to protect one bolting offspring, the others are left vulnerable. How can she solve this conundrum? Why not park the kids and charge the intruder from a distance, well before the intruder gets near her cubs? An aggressive attack, launched from a distance, engages a threat far away from the cubs. Even if the cubs scatter a bit, they are not near the confrontation and danger. To me, this explanation makes evolutionary sense, especially in rare instances when a female launches a headlong charge against a much bigger bear hundreds of meters away.

Years ago, a similar pattern of behavior was described to me by Frank Norris, a veteran ranger in Jasper National Park. While on horseback patrol in the backcountry with his wife, he sighted a big female across a wide alpine meadow. The bear gave him a quick glance and then charged straight at them, leaving her cubs behind. After dismounting and getting his wife and her horse uphill, he shot into the dirt in front of the bear. She pulled up briefly, then kept coming. Despite repeated efforts to discourage the bear, he finally killed her with a bullet to the head. She slid to a stop at his feet, dead. There seems little doubt that had he not shot her, he would have experienced serious injury or death. Again, this seemingly suicidal behavior may have worked well against other bears in an open landscape. Big males, with malicious intent toward cubs, fight back but more often respond submissively. Despite the rarity of its occurrence, this behavior presents a real challenge for maintaining the safety of visitors and park managers alike.

Orientation of the Attack

Why do bears inflict so much biting to the head and face? Grizzlies don't just grab and shake people. Some do, but all the young bears I've watched play-fighting aim their bites at the muzzle, head, and neck. The same is true with older bears when they go from play-fighting to a serious scrap. It makes sense for bears to try to control their opponent's jaws by clamping down on the muzzle, cheek, or neck, thereby preventing a return bite, because the head is held in a vise. Teeth are a bear's primary weapon. Their exceptionally long, strong claws are used mainly to dig, roll rocks, or pin down fish, but paws and claws can also be used to swat opponents or push them away. Real damage is inflicted with the massive canine teeth, which are deeply rooted in a strong, dense jawbone. The grizzly's bite is so powerful and the teeth so robust that sometimes a canine tooth is broken out of its jaw socket and left hanging. These teeth and jaws can tear flaps of flesh from a grizzly's back despite the toughness of their hide. One old male at Brooks Falls, Scar Saddle, lost a piece of skin on his back the size of a dinner plate. I suspect another big male tore the flap off in a battle over a female. It took five years for the wound to heal completely.

What explains the behavior of the attacking bear after it neutralized me? The moment Bruce yelled from behind a bush, the grizzly left me and went away over the ridge. Having subdued me—the immediate threat—perhaps her need to return to the cubs won out over dealing with another person.

Back to the Future

The tolerance of bears for people is still not grasped by those who think grizzlies equate to injury and death, especially trophy hunters. Experienced naturalist and author Doug Peacock spent much of his post-Vietnam life observing grizzly bear behavior and testing their tolerance. His colleagues sniped at his methods, alleging bear harassment when he triggered twenty-three charges as he approached bears to film them. These grizzlies did not expect people to be in the high country, where Peacock hung out. Few knew how skilled he became and the regrets he had for disturbing grizzlies. Those wilderness experiences put his war-shattered life back together. I understand the risks that copycat behavior can invite, but criticism of his endeavors is unwarranted because of his endless action to conserve wild grizzlies.

In the past, perceptions of gorillas as fearsome beasts led to killing the benign ape as a trophy for big game hunters. Enter famed zoologist Dr. George Schaller, who observed mountain gorillas in the Congo and Uganda for a pioneering behavior and ecological study from 1959–1960. It took time to recognize their benign character and complex social life. He saw that they would adapt to close approach if not threatened. After all, when Thomson's gazelles habitually associate with Chacma baboons on the African plains, we call it a type of symbiosis for mutual protection. Each species uses its best senses: gazelles hear and detect odors better, but baboons excel in using vision to warn of predators, like a stalking leopard. However, when biologists succeed in developing closer bonds with bears, it is often viewed as an unnatural event or a pathological intrusion. We might recall that Paleolithic people developed relationships with ungulates and carnivores for their benefit, and domestication followed. Is it time to advance our perceptions of grizzlies?

I know I can get along a lot better with bears if I choose to do so. Many of us are so hung up about being injured by a bear that we are overwhelmed by the notion that this mammal is extremely dangerous. Can we please get over it?

7

Too Much Is Never Enough

A land of great plenty is this Alaska of the Bears. Foods of a thousand kinds are lavishly strewn, to be had for the gathering. So that when November comes with chilly nights, with ice-bound brooks, with hillsides spreads of food no longer available, the Big Bear is fat; and, knowing when to quit, he seeks him out a den.

—Ernest Thompson Seton, *Lives of Game Animals*

The Skinny on Fat Bears

I stood on the shore of Brooks River watching what, the day before, had been a serene estuary pool but which was now alive with thousands of fish churning the two-hundred-foot-wide surface. It is mesmerizing to gaze on such a vast invasion of life concentrated in a tiny area. In late June, Pacific salmon enter Bristol Bay and flood into Katmai National Park, an area the size of Wales. It reminded me of caribou migrating across the coastal plains of Alaska, one of the greatest concentrations of animals on Earth. The possibility to observe bears catching fish looked never-ending.

As salmon entered the river, bears chased them everywhere, some wilder and crazier than others. One blond, dish-faced mother with new cubs was the drama queen. Starting her run high up on the shore, she charged toward the river. One could easily mistake this charge as being directed toward the human observer. Unnerving as her explosion of speed was, she was totally focused on fish, moving as if certain of capturing a salmon. In a blur of fur, she hit the water, leaping forward, front legs outstretched to belly flop, spread-eagle style. To her, every leap should snag a fish. Coming up short did not change her behavior. I never did see her get a fish even when the river was thick with salmon throughout July.

Watching bears is the most fun when salmon are fresh from the ocean and vigorous. One day in July, I heard the splashing of a bear racing after salmon in the nearby shallows. From my ringside viewing platform, I saw the predator pounce, pinning her slippery quarry to the bottom with long claws and dexterous paws. Then a swift bite locked a grip on the writhing salmon, which struggled and shook, causing the bear's head to wobble. She hauled the bleeding prize across the river toward a thicket right under my tower. She was so close that I froze my hand movements so as not to spook her. Less than three meters below my feet, she flopped down to strip off the salmon's fins and skin. It was my chance to see how fast a bear can devour a fish. It took only three minutes for her to finish an entire five-pound salmon. As soon as she left, I hastened to search for remains but found only blood smears and one bony gill cover, about the size of a potato chip.

Many bears eat salmon by nipping into the tough skin on the back. With dexterous incisors, they strip the skin off like a sock. In a few big bites, the flesh is mostly gone. The chilling crunches of molars on bone tells me the skeleton and head are finished. Many chases end without a catch, but fish are so abundant, thrashing through shallow water, that even the loser bears become winners.

In September, carcasses line the shore. The stench of decaying fish broadcasts salmon abundance. Bodies drift downstream as the river floods after rainstorms. This endless supply of food is just what I needed to determine how much salmon a bear can devour. Food processing (Braun bear?) may be a more appropriate term, because the endless ingestion of raw flesh is obsessive, even nauseating.

I selected one bear to follow as she caught each fish, from her first appearance until she gave up and disappeared into the forest, one and a half hours later. I tallied twenty-three salmon eaten! Since this occurred at the end of summer, the fat content of each fish was half or less of a July fish, but it still amounted to one hundred pounds of flesh. It's not hard to see how these Alaskan bears can gain over three hundred pounds of fat in a few months.

Storing body fat is essential for hibernation. Eating animal protein is important for a growing bear, but adults need fat as fuel. Adult bears often avoid ingesting muscle, preferring skin, eggs, and brains, all oily organs in a salmon. Fish filets fail as food, because muscle is costlier to digest and convert to blubber. Muscle also displaces room in the gut for greasier fare. Polar bears, who primarily survive on seals, peel and eat the sub-dermal fat, leaving muscle and innards for Arctic foxes.

Our research contract at Brooks River obliged me, as principal investigator, to document all the reactions of bears to people. A side benefit was endless opportunities to watch the methods bears use to catch fish. In 1970, Mike Luque, a student from Utah State University, described how the ineffective capture techniques used by some bears at McNeil Falls did not improve over time. When food rewards are high, bears appear to learn immediately from one experience, even a botched-up job satisfies, and then add that practice to their repertoire. Could fast learners be benefitting from observing others? If so, a local behavioral culture should develop and lead those fatter bears to survive at higher numbers. I explore that intriguing avenue a bit later in this book.

Hard-wired for Overeating

Grizzly bears astound biologists with the vast range of food items and quantities taken. We might expect all large carnivores to specialize in large prey, given that cougars and African lions specialize in deer and antelope. But grizzlies are generalists, eating hundreds of items, many as small as moths, ants, bee larvae, and Whitebark pine nuts. I am perplexed by the amount of energy it takes to dig up small rodents and tiny roots. This eclectic diet hints at their strategy for success. Unlike big cats, who rest eighteen hours a day, grizzlies have been observed chomping and chewing up to eighteen hours per day on the sunny slopes of Denali National Park in central Alaska. However, salmon top the list of favored foods anywhere they can be caught. The bonanza of spawning salmon in summer and fall may have brought on a more social disposition in Alaskan bears. Such a consistent, massive concentration of food should produce a less-aggressive bear, making them more tolerant of each other. This tolerance can extend to humans. We can choose to reciprocate.

A bear's life revolves around finding food. A large, active, big-brained omnivore needs constant fueling. When fall arrives, hyperphasia, a physiological imperative, drives bears to pack on blubber for life in the den. With such unrelenting hunger, splashing salmon electrify bears.

So far, Alaska's coastal parks have benefitted from a rich supply of fish that enter undammed rivers, pristine lakes, and their tributaries. Katmai may be the largest protected bear factory in the world, surpassing Russia's remote, salmon-rich Kamchatka Peninsula. In a comparison of population studies of Alaska's bears, the density of Katmai bears ranked far above all the others. What is it about this landscape that is so good for bears? I found out, because good fortune set me down in Alaska's best habitat for grizzlies, such an intriguing contrast to my experience in Yellowstone's cold, high landscape.

A combination of factors make salmon a superior food for bear survival, especially compared to other foods. First, salmon are large, abundant, and concentrated. Their renewal rate or replacement outpaces foods like berries, which are gone when a patch is exploited. The conveyor belt of salmon is not depleted much over the four-month period of salmon runs. Second, salmon concentrations are highly predictable in space and time, a plus for a bright animal with a big appetite. Third, salmon are easily captured in shallow riffles or waterfall obstructions. Once a bear locates a school of salmon, it can quit searching and concentrate on catching. Finally, prolonged availability means salmon surpass fruit and berries, which has to be eaten as they ripen, or else they drop off or are taken by others. Salmon are available fresh, or not so fresh, from July through October. These facts have far-reaching implications for how we can relate to grizzlies more safely and sanely.

Katmai's rich salmon watersheds outclass other sites in Alaska and coastal BC. Brooks River bears can feed for four months on one huge run of sockeye salmon. Brooks Falls is two days from the sea, as fish swim. Bears are there in July to meet the silvery horde. These fish are fat with fuel for an arduous migration, vigorous nest building, courting, and finally, aggressive nest defense and mating. Salmon rank high in nutrition for bears, because fish oils are energy rich, easily digested, and assimilate rapidly into fat. Such a diet contrasts sharply with sedge, which carries bears marginally through the spring. A close relative of grass, sedge, is high in protein when young but not easily digested at maturity because of its woody cell walls. With a carnivore's gut, bears don't gain weight on sedge salad.

As the sockeye surged upriver, I was always mesmerized by the extravaganza sweeping under the floating bridge on Brooks River. To photograph this bonanza, mostly hidden beneath the surface, I waited until panic made hundreds thrash wildly at the surface. Their finny backs glistened in the sunlight, giving a wide-angle view of densely packed schools. This "salmon jam" brought the description of Lewis and Clark to mind—salmon so dense that one could walk across the river on their backs.

Schools surged upriver, holding below the falls. On the rocky lip of the falls, hungry bears staked out their turf. Some had preferred fishing spots, a pattern that persisted through July. Others searched below the falls in the churning froth that tumbled fish to the surface. From the deeper pools, fish erupted airborne to land in the smooth water cascading over the falls. In the deepest pool, an old, scarred male grizzly, Diver, submerged for a full minute to lunge at fish. Techniques for catching salmon seem infinite. Most common is "snorkeling," where only the ears of a walking bear are visible, perhaps to maintain vigilance.

Fishing at the falls was the curtain opener to many acts in a summer featuring salmon for four months. Bears unable to compete at the falls picked up injured fish that were stunned on rocks during a leap and carried downstream in the current. Our data sheets filled quickly with numbers, timing of captures, and social interactions of bears at the falls. As July waned, bears were visibly fatter and markedly less aggressive as fish numbers tapered off. Salmon that escaped snapping jaws continued upstream into Brooks Lake and its tributaries. In shallow, gravelly creeks, salmon competed, displayed, and built nest depressions for spawning. Gone was their silver sheen, replaced by green heads and vivid red bodies. Once again, these fish faced more predation from the same bears they had evaded at Brooks Falls.

To test the idea that bears commute to these streams, we searched for a major bear trail beside Brooks Lake in the direction of the tributaries. Bear trails are easy to identify. My student, Scott Fitkin, and I had already tallied fifty-five minor bear trails crossing the two-kilometer road between Naknek Lake and Brooks Lake.

I found one unusually deep trail that was strikingly different from the others. It ran parallel to the shore of Brooks Lake, leading directly toward many tributaries without side branches. Being so well formed meant it had been established long earlier. No bear trail I had ever seen had such a deep U-shaped depression, devoid of vegetation with vertical edges surrounded by green, spongy sphagnum moss. It was similar to deeply carved elk trails in Yellowstone Park, created by annual migrations over mountain passes. Unlike elk trails, which are narrow and hoof-chewed, this bear trail was evenly formed, and wide bear paws and elk hooves had left their millennial code, reminders of lost wonders in wounded landscapes. Sculpted by the footfalls of countless bears silently passing over the centuries, this was the bear highway of my dreams. Another piece of the puzzle fell into place!

The end of spawning and nest defense became obvious when the river filled with exhausted and decaying salmon. Astonishing masses of animal flesh collected downriver, salmon carcasses piling up like driftwood in eddies and becoming lodged in long grass bordering the river. Carcasses lined the shore like paving stones. This cornucopia of corpses occurs when bears are completing their hyperphagic phase, which builds fat deposits to sustain them over winter. In the den, that fat is metabolized to produce energy and water. Consuming dead or dying fish is the third phase of the four-month period of continuous access to salmon. As I watched bears being choosey about these morsels, I saw them sniff and reject fish with little residual fat. But I also saw carcasses with skulls opened by bear incisors, their brain tissue neatly extracted. The fat content of brain matter is 55 percent phospholipid, a complex fat. This makes sense: the millions of brain neurons are enclosed in a fatty sheath, like the plastic insulation on electrical cable. Although the fish's body has lost all its fat, not so the brain, with nerve trunks to sense organs. Although the fish burn stored fat for body maintenance during reproduction, they cannot sacrifice their computer, useful to the end of life. Bears probably can smell concentrated fats for selective feeding on these fatty morsels. Their taste system may also be anatomically biased toward fats, oils, and waxes that are easily converted into body stores. Bears focus their feeding so much on fat-laden foods, such as Whitebark pine nuts, bee larvae, moths, and beetles, that I categorize bears as "lipophiles," fat lovers.

For many years, we continued our research late into the fall at Katmai, primarily to see if new bears arrived after the generators were shut down and visitors left. This stage also enabled observation of the final feeding phase on dead salmon. Of all the food-finding techniques, the most startling was to witness bears swimming out into deep water to get carcasses that had been washed into Naknek Lake. From the beach on a chilly morning, I noticed a big bear offshore in about ten feet of water. At that depth, he stood with his hind legs touching the bottom. At first, I thought he might be using his hind feet to kick salmon up to his front paws, as I'd seen in the deeper part of the river. But this bear pushed up off the bottom, then ducked, head first, down to the bottom. These are such water-loving bears that I imagined this as a beginning stage in the evolution of the polar bear. This diving technique added a new feeding niche, extending the phase that salmon were accessible to bears. Innovative feeding behavior also confers a fitness benefit to problem-solving bears. It is also the kind of behavior that other bears can observe, thus establishing a tradition. The collection of fish-harvesting tricks suggested how Brooks River bears had become so big, fat and numerous. As a group, they had figured out every possible way to capitalize on one big run of sockeye salmon, using it from mid-summer until snow and cold called them to their high-country dens. Relying on massive salmon migrations with skills developed for following fish throughout their migrations resulted, no doubt, in high den survival. In fact, that survival was indicated in the spring by the appearance of heavy bears carrying fat reserves not utilized during denning.

What is it about the intelligence of these bears that facilitates discovery of salmon movement over the landscape? Many biologists have commented on bears' ability to move quickly to known locations, especially bears transported away from capture sites. For example, in 1972, Yellowstone biologist Glen Cole told me that grizzlies captured and relocated had outrun the transport vehicles back to the capture site. Wolves can return directly to their den from any spot in their territory using a "cognitive map," a mapping skill with no need for memorizing environmental cues or following the same route back to a den. If bears can navigate directly to fish concentrations using such memory capability, it would have significant survival value. Being first to exploit arriving fish has a huge advantage. Consider the space and time challenges for a bear. Salmon are distributed in patches, their occurrence ephemeral in time, especially at an obstruction like a waterfall. If a bear failed to coordinate with salmon arrival, it risked failure to survive denning. A bear remembering how to pinpoint salmon has an abundant, readily available, and renewable food source. All these ecological factors about salmon runs account for the dense aggregations of grizzly bears.

Abundant and easily accessible food makes these bears less aggressive toward one another. Their more sociable behavior differs from Rocky Mountain grizzlies, which are more food limited and thus less tolerant than salmon bears. Just as Yellowstone grizzlies are aggressive to competitors, like wolves, they may also be more intolerant of people and quicker to threaten or charge. This is speculation, albeit highly informed. Until more systematic research is done on these questions, the best we have is circumstantial evidence of causes based on differences documented by long-term direct observation. When bears can exploit enormous numbers of fat-rich fish, there is no advantage to being prickly about your real estate. Aggressive behavior interrupts foraging and risks injury. There is no question that bears compete for fishing rights, but they so do more frequently at the beginning of the run, when the bears are hungrier and fewer fish are available. Later it's all pigging out. Ignore your neighbor!

Our detailed records and photography of known individuals paid real dividends regarding bear navigation and memory. When graduate student (and later park resource scientist) Tamara Olson was completing her thesis study at Brooks Camp, she learned to recognize about thirty bears over the course of her fieldwork. Being on the river throughout the daylight hours permitted her to follow every bear for some period during each week, making notes, drawings, and recording first and last appearances of known individuals. In her third fall at Brooks, she reviewed her data and found that one female suddenly appeared for the first time on September 28 three years in a row. At no time was this female seen in the summer or fall, only coming to fish late in the season. Maybe she disliked the crowds and fed elsewhere early on. What amazed me was her ability to navigate to the same place on the same date three years in a row. We have no idea how far she came or whether she used cues, like the sounds of generators, to tell the time of the year. In late September, a smaller generator was substituted, so a different sound could be a clue heard from a distance. It was not unusual to note new arrivals at the river in the fall after the commercial camp shut down.

Some of these bears were unhappy encountering humans on trails late in the season, so we took extra precautions and recalibrated our cocky attitude of "knowing" what bears would do.

Heavy Bears and Water Beds

The massive size of bears in late autumn at Brooks was astonishing. They weren't just large but clinically obese. Some old adult males were absolutely pear shaped, their bellies nearly dragging on the ground, their back and legs padded with fat. Supporting all that weight when sleeping on hard ground, even sand, had to be uncomfortable, judging from the bear-sized depressions they dug into the beach, large enough to cushion a bear's belly. This may have been for immediate comfort or an adaptation to prevent blood clots. Like humans getting bedsores, I assumed the reason bears prepared these daybeds was to ease pressure, so nerves or blood vessels were not blocked. Similar depressions are found in grizzly bears dens into which I have crawled, so this seems a year-round habit.

One afternoon along Brooks River, I saw one bear's solution to relieve foot pressure. An older bear, Diver, was being his usual aquatic self, immersed in water. Then I noticed he was unusually still, tucked up against an island in the estuary. Standing in water over his shoulders, he dropped his head on a grassy bank, dead asleep. Being totally supported, he had the bear version of a waterbed, with the advantage of being near his food supply. Being large, he had no need to scurry off into the woods for a secure bed. Nobody messed with Diver.

Diver astonished me with another sleeping trick. I watched him from an overlook, hoping to pinpoint his fish-capture rate. His head went down into the water for a time, like a bear searching for fish, but he came up with nothing. Nor did he seem to be moving. He was nodding in sleep, nose raised for a breath every so often. There's no end to efficiency and comfort in adaptable Yogi.

8

Thinking Like A Grizzly

From the pervasive stench of rotten fish, we knew autumn had arrived at Brooks River. Thousands of spawned-out salmon had washed downstream and were being hauled ashore and dismembered by seventy bears, their last feast before retreating to their dens. In the river shallows and back eddies, fungus-coated fish lay in piles. Gradually, carcasses and parts flushed into Naknek Lake, where currents carried them in front of Brooks Camp. On the shore beside the lodge, I watched bears dive down or kick them up with their feet.

From the trail, I glimpsed a familiar female as she dove for sunken treasure. Her two cubs ambled along the shore more or less abreast of her. They were no longer bawling anxiously at her, as they did early in the season. The cubs were like spirited puppies, exploring everything along their path but ever aware of their guardian's location.

I grabbed my camera and tripod to record their behavior near people. I was curious to see how this bear, separated from her cubs, remained alert to threats. Out in four to five feet of water, she moved along slowly. She may have learned that dead salmon wash out into the lake from her past snorkeling in the river, her eyes submerged to locate remaining fish. As the cubs moved in on me, my enthusiasm faded to concern.

How would mom react? I watched her face for alarm signals when she glanced my way. No stare, no woof, no throat clicks to tell her cubs to shape up. She just kept searching. I moved back into the woods, because the cubs had seen me. Even knowing this bear's tolerance, I granted the cubs space, so as not to set a poor example for others watching this little drama. I was also thinking of the long term. Close approaches encourage cubs to become familiar with people, which can lead to over-assertiveness if their behavior escalates to cheeky dominance as teenagers.

I packed my camera away and walked back to my tent, treading silently on wet birch leaves. While passing the ranger station, a snapping branch directed me to a bear nonchalantly crossing camp to get to the river, close enough that his wet-dog rankness enveloped me. I passed by with thoughts about the many habituated moms with cubs and images of conflicts to be. Did we have risky, defensive females or calm moms that used humans as shields to park their kids near? The complex and startling reality was that bears acted appropriately as the situation demanded. The tolerant mother was also the fearless defender when a big male threatened. So, instead of thinking of bear spray as brains in a can, we can smell the coffee about this intelligent animal and recognize that understanding the context and location of encounters makes for a safer and more bear-compatible world.

Seemingly harmless interactions with bears play into a visitor's dreamy sense of oneness with them. Close approach to bears can transform normal shyness into boldness when the bear later approaches people seeking food. This has the same effect as dropping a lunch pack to distract a bear from following you. The next person has to deal with a bear you trained to approach people, which never ends well for the bear. If we keep restraint in mind when approaching a wild bear, we are respecting its wildness. No matter how much a person appreciates an animal's intelligence, we must leave teaching them to ride a bicycle to the circus folk.

Why Are Brooks Bears So Tolerant of People?

When I first stepped off a floatplane onto the beach at Brooks Camp on a beautiful fall day in 1983, I came with memories from my nasty encounter in Yellowstone, six years earlier. My recent experience with black bears in Yosemite park and elsewhere, plus literature on wildlife-people conflicts filled many gaps in my knowledge about grizzly bears encountering people on salmon streams.

The lore about old silver-tip seemed to be a patchwork of stereotypes, repeated over and over: "They attack without warning; their behavior is complex and totally unpredictable; they kill for pleasure." A ship's captain knows that fierce storms can be unpredictable if you don't study the sky, winds, and wave action. The fact is, with more people among fewer and fewer bears, it is harder and harder to learn about grizzlies. A few exceptional people, like my friends Doug Peacock and Brian Horejsi, have gotten to know grizzlies well, the same way Adolph Murie got to know Denali grizzlies—through years of observation at close range with an open mind.

My research specialty was ethology, the scientific study of behavior of wild, free-ranging animals (not handled or marked). With thirty-five years of firsthand field observation, I felt suitably prepared to interpret grizzly behavior, salted with some disciplined speculation, as appropriate. Speculation, when viewed as a temporary hypothesis, can be a stepping-stone to help unravel knotty questions.

Let's go back to innovations in bears, like learning to dive for salmon in lakes. The behavior mirrors that of chimps and wolves when an individual finds a new food source, learns to capture it, and transmits the trait to offspring. This satisfies the definition of a cultural trait seen in other big-brained animals. Gaining access to dead salmon washed into the lake bottom introduced a new food niche for bears to exploit and store in their pre-frontal lobes. Finding lake-bottom carcasses late in the season adds dessert to a big-dinner summer. Besides being a food source without competitors (and associated risks), this is more payoff long after carcasses in the river are depleted. The extension of the fattening-up period significantly enhances den survival. The genius of grizzlies is evident in their discovery of places and seasons where abundant food is available, then stored in memory, an adaptation that certainly contributes to the huge size of Brooks bears. Dead salmon were the clean-up act in their four-month exploitation of the sockeye population. No matter where the salmon went, starting with the early runs of sea-bright, fat-packed fish to the distant shallow spawning streams, then back to the falls, where spawned-out "stinkers" abounded, bears had learned all the sites of fish concentration. The backbone of a successful animal "culture" is the triumph of learning, memory, and transmitting knowledge to the next generation.

How did we explain the baffling tolerance of these bears around people? Katmai bear behavior seems to clash with observations of grizzlies elsewhere. This fascinating adaptation of bears to people probably involved all the following events and processes.

Brooks River has been superior breeding habitat for salmon for thousands of years, even though shallow water and a fish-defying waterfall make them vulnerable to capture. Could these bears have drifted genetically to be less aggressive, allowing more time to prey on salmon? Aggression for territorial defense risks injury and reduces their catch of super-abundant but transient fish. Evolutionary theory supports a tolerance of social adaptation. Greater tolerance between bears was transferred to people, where the people were not harming the bears. At least that was the simplest interpretation, to my mind.

I have observed female bears tolerating people near their cubs many times. Wherever bears have lived for millennia among people, especially around tribes that harvest salmon, mutual tolerance has developed. Current protection of bears from hunting and minimizing disturbance encourages these "ferocious" grizzlies to respond much more tolerantly.

Indeed, rangers at Brooks told visitors that these bears were warier of other bears than they were of us.

The rapid development of tolerance may have begun as a behavioral variant of an individual, later incorporated genetically as a generally tolerant disposition. Alternatively, the Brooks River regulars could be a small segment of the population that accepted whatever hassle came with fishing among lots of bears and people.

Relatively unproductive habitat (like Yellowstone) set the stage for intolerance among bears. Territorial aggression paid off when animals were food stressed, and that intolerance carried over to people, to some extent. Added to crankiness brought on by hunger, mountain bears have been injured or threatened by humans near hunting camps, cabins, and ranches. Hunters and recreationists on ATVs have crisscrossed an expanding networks of forestry roads in grizzly habitat, each with rifles racked and ready to dispatch coyote, lion or bear. Over decades bears, have been captured in snares or culvert traps by wildlife biologists, which has not endeared man to them.

Consider the ethical implications of all this for grizzly bear management. Biologists capture problem bears and transplant them to distant locations, far enough to inhibit a bear's return. This way, the reasoning goes, another population of bears is augmented, avoiding euthanization or confinement in a zoo. But the problem bear, conditioned to human fare, becomes a victim transported to lands unknown, where finding food aggravates his multiple stresses. Lastly, if the transplanted bear is released onto another bear's turf, he or she will be attacked as an intruder. For research-captured grizzlies in the Yellowstone ecosystem, this handling represents thirty-five years of mistreatment for hundreds of bears.

Any resulting fear or wariness from the overkill of grizzly bears in the 1970s could be transmitted by the bears that escaped the killing. Over 220 grizzlies died at the hands of humans following the closure of dumps. This transmission process is discussed in more detail below.

Changing Grizzly Bear Culture

Bears are allegedly being "tamed" when they become habituated to people. Their wildness, critics claim, is artificially modified by "unnatural" contacts with park managers or throngs of people. The faulty assumption lurking here is that the natural behavior of wild creatures is immediate flight upon detecting people. But why should the natural response of animals to humans be flight? African antelopes do not flee from lions unless they are being stalked or chased. The same goes for caribou with wolves. If prey animals raced off at every predator encounter, the cost in energy for their nervousness would be unsustainable. In reality, they detect a predator's motivation and habituate to them when they are not a threat. Similarly, at Brooks River, the protected grizzlies learned that people were harmless, so they conserved energy by adapting to benign human activity.

Innovation and Culture: Mom and Cubs

If we understood the extent of the knowledge that a bear accumulates through learning, like locating disparate seasonal foods, we would appreciate that survival depends on this cultural knowledge, grounded on a profound memory capacity. Bears are tightly linked to their habitat by memory of learned and socially transmitted behavior. Given the variability of seasonal foods, such as berries and nuts, it requires years to learn where they occur and, more importantly, what alternatives are available in years of fruit or seed failures. Yellowstone's grizzly-management specialists have recently compiled lists of food items eaten by park bears from seventy years of studies. About one thousand species of plants and animals are on the menu.

Now consider the plight of a Yellowstone grizzly trying to adapt to alternate foods, when preferred foods like Whitebark pine nuts, trout, and ungulate carcasses have declined or disappeared. Government biologists were sure that bears could switch to any of the thousand or so other small items that have been identified in bear scats. Why were bears not already eating this stuff in quantity? It might well be due to insufficient nutrient content. It looks like bears have suffered from assumptions that are good for politics and bad for bears.

Bear Behavior Changed by Rewards or Punishment

Earlier I pointed to the variability in aggressive behavior of grizzlies toward people in national parks and suggested how our treatment of them affects their reactions. The most tolerant bears have learned that benign human contacts are not threatening. The clearest examples are in large national parks, like Katmai, where bears have been protected from hunting and capture.

One exception to the rapid habituation model came from black bear studies in Rocky Mountain National Park, carried out by my late friend, Hank McCutchen. In the 1960s, he studied an unusual population of thirty to thirty-five bears that lived at high elevation there. They were uncharacteristically nocturnal in activity and shy in response to human contact. Over one hundred years, these bears had been shot outside this small park. More recently, bears raiding garbage or damaging property were relocated or destroyed. Hank explained in a letter to me that these high-elevation bears had long ago learned to avoid people and our calorie-rich garbage. The result was lower body weights in adults and cubs, which sometimes starved, because they could not find sufficient food in that high, cold habitat. One explanation for such reclusive behavior involves a new cultural pattern that began with learned behavior that then advanced to genetic changes in the population. Other larger black bears at lower elevations nearby did not display this behavior. They were not subjected to the same killing, removal, or harassment experiences, because they stayed out of trouble and remained protected.

Mammals like dolphins, elephants, wolves, and grizzly bears are capable of rapid behavioral change or cultural evolution, because learned skills can be imprinted into every generation. As with humans, this involves a capacity to innovate responses to the environment that are unavailable through slower genetic change. I am not proposing a new process here, only noting that wildlife researchers often consider only classical genetic models in their concern for isolated grizzly populations. This was reasonable for fruit fly genetic adaptation, but that model is too restrictive. Bears have adapted behaviorally rather quickly but only slowly genetically. Here is how that might have worked.

A new paradigm might show how grizzlies respond to changes in food resources, from climate change to deadly contacts with humans. The current method to address genetic isolation is to introduce new bears. This may be insufficient if it is the only conservation strategy. We know that small island populations of mammals have survived and thrived, starting from a few cats, rats, or rabbits. Another illustrative example of an extremely inbred species is the African cheetah. It has not gone extinct despite its limited gene pool. When planning for grizzly conservation, bear managers could enlarge their tactical toolbox to include behavioral adaptation. For example, if research handling of grizzly bears has caused them to avoid better habitat near people, then the cost is hungrier bears predisposed to kill livestock.

The invasion of grizzly habitat by well-armed humans has been the equivalent of a super predator invading an island. This approach requires a different historical perspective of grizzly bear survival in North America. The bear, as a former top predator, was ill-prepared for the destructive onslaught of traps, poison and guns brought on by trappers and settlers. Bears now occupy habitat islands too small to avoid periodic destruction on all the borders. Even when bears have legal protection under the Endangered Species Act, the level of mortality reaches unsustainable levels. So, how can grizzlies survive when they no longer have that protection? They might become reclusive, occupy remote high country, and evolve smaller bodies, like the relict brown bears of Europe. Or they could go extinct. Their fate is in the hands of the super predator, *Homo not-so-sapiens*.

Conservation strategists need to know if capturing grizzlies shortens their fuse in encounters with hikers. There were at least two incidences of grizzlies killing people while recovering from anesthetics. How a bear's behavior changed after drugging might depend on the intensity of psychological stress and physical pain from the process. Minimal effects of darting of McNeil and Brooks River bears in the 1960s were reported. However, the influence of many frequent benign interactions with non-threatening people may account for the rapid return of the captured bears to fishing in the river. Some darted animals were unaware of the biologists' presence before being drugged, so if no human was immediately visible when they recovered, the bears would not be able to associate humans with any pain or unpleasantness.

When trapped bears have fought to get free, they have injured their legs in snares or broken teeth from chewing cables or biting at steel cage mesh in culvert traps. I have examined such damage in skulls and have assumed that the pain experienced by bears would be linked to humans. As a matter of fact, simulated capture and handling procedures were used as an aversive technique by managers to discourage bears from approaching people and our stuff. As a hiker in Yellowstone, I do not want to meet a bear that has been captured six times. Because this impact has not been studied, we can anticipate injuries and related lawsuits will be one consequence of our continued ignorance. I agree with a growing clan of biologists in the Yellowstone ecosystem who want the trapping of research bears replaced with non-intrusive techniques, such as trail cameras, direct observations, and hair-trapped DNA. Let the wild ones keep their wildness.

When we realize much of an animal's behavior derives from individual experience, we have considered the brain of large mammals to be like a computer, programmed by early experiences and different from the more rigid behavior patterns seen in fish or reptiles. Animals with much smaller brains are clearly capable of certain kinds of learning but are not plastic enough to vary much between generations. I envision our animal world consisting of those species with robotic, hard-wired behavior and the newer others with greater flexibility in their behavioral repertoire. An example of the latter is killer whales feeding on different prey and having various dialects in their communication that are specific to each social group. Similar examples can be drawn from wolves, apes, and elephants. So far, we have not considered bears, perhaps because they appear to be not as social. But my experience of the bonds between mothers and young, siblings, and coalitions of sub-adult bears provides extensive opportunities for development of social variation in their intelligent lives.

When environmental opportunities exist for rapid learning and social transmission of valuable new skills, the bear culture begins to shift, a form of micro-evolution. Finding new, more rewarding food niches, for example, increases survival value, and those innovators dominate the population over time. The opposite appears to have happened with Rocky Mountain National Park's black bears. Their separation from the larger low-elevation bears suggests the culture of these small bears may go extinct.

9

Bears Can Fake It

Anatomy of a Bluff Charge

Grizzly buffs know what a bluff charge looks like, but its cause and meaning have remained mysterious. The very term rings of devious behavior or uncertainty in a bear confronting a threat. When an explosive charge stops precipitously or the bear diverts to the side at the last minute, we label this a bluff charge. Often the bear's front feet slam into the ground, braking its momentum. Forward-directed ears and a raised body posture during this behavior suggest the bear's motivation is wavering or it is conflicted about proceeding. I filmed one complete sequence of an interaction that proved instructive.

It was early in July on Brooks River, when enormous runs of salmon began throughout the long, warm summer days. No matter how carefully I crossed the floating bridge on the way to my lookout, the river's surface exploded with sockeye, briefly panicked on their way upstream. A wave of thrashing bodies whipped the river's glassy surface from shore to shore. Bears were converging on the river with one thing in mind: fish.

From my fifteen-foot perch, I caught sight of my favorite bear family, a large blond female and two small cubs, who were weaving in and out of the grass on the riverbank. She walked downstream in about a foot of water, searching the muddy shoreline for fish, then passed the floating bridge and headed toward a shrubby island in the estuary. I climbed down to get ahead of the family, whose midday appearance in the estuary was rare. This scenario had promise for one of my objectives: to see how bear families respond to people and how people react to a family of bears. With some luck, I hoped to get a video sequence for fine-grained analysis of any interactions. Even a bear-on-bear confrontation would be worthwhile. I was warming to the prospect and to the sunny morning, especially after leaving my cold, windowless, wall tent. It was pure joy to hike the paths around Brooks River anticipating the people-bear circus.

For my camera set-up, I chose an old wharf on the lakeshore well ahead and above where the bear family seemed to be heading. Right on schedule, the female popped out of the shrubbery and walked straight toward me. What luck. My adrenaline surged. From the opposite shore came a skinny sub-adult bear aimed right toward the family. This looked like a suicidal move. What the hell was going on? Mom continued walking forward, cubs in tow. I turned on my camera to capture any initial events if a rapid sequence followed.

About two meters below my platform, the sub-adult waded toward the family group. In the viewfinder, I saw the female glance back at the cubs and then charge toward the sub-adult. He spun back into the shallow water. The instant the sub-adult turned, the female accelerated into a headlong charge. Immediately, the sub-adult squatted, urinating as he half turned to face her. Later replay of the sequences showed a bear as thoroughly intimidated as any bear I've ever seen. The skinny little guy was butt to face with an angry mom but turned to face her at the last moment to defend against bites.

Mom rushed in, roaring, then braked and looked back at her cubs. The cubs stood on their hind legs, riveted by the action. She turned, ambled back to collect her cubs, then charged the sub-adult once again. This time her galloping charge caused skinny boy to flee back into the water that he had just exited. She was so close to me that my microphone picked up the flopping sounds coming from the flapping skin and fat on her hind legs. The videotape showed her charge into the water as she closed in. Her jaws were wide open, coming within inches of his, though they never connected. For a second, they roared at each other, noses almost touching, then abruptly separated. Mom ran back to her cubs, and the sub-adult got the message: bugger off! Whatever their relationship—perhaps he was a former cub of hers—the sub-adult knew the relationship was over. He headed off so close to the dilapidated dock on which I was standing that I was afraid he was going to take his frustration out on me. (Sometimes a dominated bear bullies another to regain status by threatening a subordinate.) Luckily for me, not that day. He walked on and disappeared into a clump of trees.

As I stopped the camera, I noticed my hands were shaking. A flashback of an attacking grizzly had kicked in momentarily but was soon followed by excitement and satisfaction with the filming coup. I only missed a small segment, because I lost my nerve when the charging bear came too close. I had visualized this melee ending up in my lap. Everything broke out so fast, and with my only eye in the viewfinder, I could not determine where the scrap was going. Still, I had captured dramatic footage of the sub-adult male's behavior, which taught a potent lesson. Don't run, or you'll provoke a charge. I assumed the smaller bear was trying to re-establish a relationship with his mother, but she was having none of it. The big revelation for me was the split-second reaction between the two, instantly adjusting behavior to that of the other. So, if you are confronting a cheeky bear, stand still with your bear spray at the ready. I tried the run-away tactic once. It did not work—I took a licking.

Years later at Knight Inlet Lodge on the BC coast, a similarly astonishing response by a mother bear reacting to a motionless person sitting on the ground was photographed. An amateur photographer decided to risk sitting beside an active bear trail, a practice not tolerated among lodge guests. A naturalist-guide, Michelle McLellan, standing in a platform nearby, took photos of the sequence. The curious mother's expressions were intriguing as she approached the man, who remained frozen. Slide one showed her walking calmly down the trail toward him, trailing a year-old cub. When about five feet away, she sniffed his pack and then his tripod but still did not see him. The next photo shows the man squatting, his head less than a half a meter from her jaws. At that moment, she was staring right at him, ears cocked forward, her big frying-pan paw raised, ready to swat him. Just then Michelle yelled at her, and she quickly lowered her paw and calmly turned and walked back the way she came, her cub still in tow. This was an astonishingly swift reversal from an alarm response to calm withdrawal. If Michelle had not called out, there's no telling how it would have ended. But the mom was tolerant as long as the person stayed still.

Can Bears Fake Aggression?

After reviewing films of aggressive behavior, and being at the receiving end of some, I detected an ambivalence in charge sequences that looks like rapid mood changes in bears. I am speculating about a bear's capacity for deviousness, but the volatility in the island mom's rapid escalation of her charge well after she noticed the other bear and then inhibition of bites in the jaw-to-jaw drama made calling it a bluff seem appropriate. If she were truly aggressive on seeing the smaller bear approaching, she would have charged right away and snapped at or bitten him. But she reacted to his submission while retreating and gauged the degree of her threat sufficient to get the desired result. The other option is to consider these changes as rapid mood sequences. Either way, volatility is the rule, but the behavior looked to be under minute-to-minute control.

The fact that the sub-adult bear insisted on approaching the female with cubs suggested to me that she was his mother. His itch to join her was clearly not reciprocated. Maybe pushy photographers could learn from this and keep a situation from escalating by judicious retreat.

The term "bluff charge" suggests uncertainty or hoodwinking, although a charge could simply be a trial move by a conflicted bear. As bears mature, they commonly assert themselves with other bears. It is one way they find out how big and bad they are, or the reverse. All outcomes provide useful information for growing bears. With growth in size comes the potential to dominate in conflict situations. What we call aggressive behavior may be switched on or off at a more conscious level. The mom displayed just enough bravado to convince the smaller bear that his approach was unwanted. She communicated that the old bond was finished, but without any painful punishment. She moderated her rejection for the desired effect. This seems consistent with bears' cognitive ability. When cubs play, they inhibit their bites. Understanding this capacity can help us avoid unpleasant encounters by being less fearful and more tolerant.

Another explanation for "bluff charges" is a tendency to charge at the unknown and then switch to a more nuanced response as more information is gained. This is consistent with my observations of reversals of chasing, especially by sub-adult bears, as the antagonists discover who is bigger or more aggressive.

The recorded charge shows the tight control of the female's biting behavior. In the final confrontation, the sub-adult turned to face her, likely to protect his rear when she got within biting range. He matched her jaw-to-jaw with a bellowing roar. She seemed to be saying, "I'd bite you if I could do it without getting bitten back." This looks like she ratcheted up the bluff to provoke the desired withdrawal behavior .

I marveled at how the mother keyed her behavior to the subtle changes in the sub-adult's response. This showed how rapidly mood intensity can be modulated. For a human surprise encounter, this means the outcome has a lot to do with how a person responds. Bears are not locked into one sequence of aggressive behavior, as we imagine a shark might behave when preying on a seal. Any time during a bear's approach, a person's actions affect the bear's next series of behaviors, giving him or her many options for safe disengagement.

A Big Bear's Bluff

A stone's throw upstream from my tree stand, an older fisherman worked his way down the middle of the stream, focused on casting a fly. Coming downstream a bit faster was a local favorite, Sahale. Her big head swung back and forth as she waded with the current and closed in on the oblivious angler. I felt a strong urge to yell at him, but I had decided earlier that my job was to record these interactions and behave like I was not there. Besides, I expected the guy to wake up despite his blind and deaf act.

Before I could even whistle, Sahale rose on her hind legs and lifted her paws high, all in one motion. As she threw her massive paws toward the guy, she let out a brief explosive roar, then calmly dropped to all fours and resumed fishing. I was thunderstruck. She carried out the performance like it was a scripted bluff to be applied whenever needed. She displayed no jaw chomping or laid-back ears, nor was the hair on her back raised. It was a display of control by a good actor. The angler stumbled and fled from the river, perhaps in fear, but also maybe to change his underwear.

Give Tolerance a Chance

From all the bears' explosive but benign interactions, lessons exist to increase our safety. I was impressed with how the female's charge on the sub-adult flared up. When he turned away, the matriarch reacted as if her moves were choreographed. The same could apply to our confrontations with grizzlies. Never run when you see a bear, because running triggers a charge. Even moose know this. I recall watching a moose cross Brooks River near a fishing bear. When the moose entered the river, it was moving quickly. On seeing the bear, it slowed to a walk, though it continued to cross. When it reached the forest edge, it reverted to a faster gait and disappeared.

We can also take a page from naturalist Doug Peacock's playbook: stand perfectly still. The best outcome is the bear not seeing you. Bears have excellent vision to detect moving objects at great distances but not for picking out a still pattern against a complex background. When a grizzly sees you standing still, you most likely will elicit interest but no reaction. By running, you define yourself as something resembling a frightened subordinate—or the bear equivalent to a hamburger. Neither results in a favorable outcome. Besides, if you stand with bear spray at the ready, you are not only showing (or faking) confidence but have also communicated that you are ready to defend yourself.

Another spinoff from my video sequences was capturing the lead-in facial expressions and body postures that preceded a clash. It was the anatomy of a close encounter, a play-by-play demonstration of bear language that suggests safety tips to make people more comfortable around grizzlies. That sequence was included in the taped series of human-bear encounters that I had promised the NPS.

Are there deeper aesthetic and philosophical meanings for us, beyond the immediate application of behavioral insights? As Doug Peacock has convincingly argued in his brilliant synthesis, *In the Shadow of the Sabertooth*, our current relationship and interactions with brainy bears offer new insights about early human life among bears. His perspective arises from a life spent observing and filming wild grizzlies at close range with respect.

The measured response of the Glendale mom approaching the dim-witted photographer sitting on the ground provides a useful illustration of how subtle and calm a bear, even a female with a cub, can be when accustomed to non-threatening people, despite the extremely startling nature of the situation. This insight should give us hope that if we tolerate close interaction with grizzlies, we can coexist with them. Applied to national park roadsides, where grizzlies spawn bear jams, further tolerance for benign interactions with habituated bears is possible. As mentioned, it may require that we replace traditional capture and collaring techniques with less-intrusive hair capture and video camera practices. Canadian wildlife ecologist Marc Caddet and others have demonstrated that current capturing procedures have more harmful physical and physiological impacts on bears than previously assumed. No doubt further work will add more negative behavioral consequences.

The amazing capacity of this creature's adaptive traits may reveal why Native Americans watched grizzlies, learned survival tricks from them, and considered them sacred. They admired them for their formidable ability to find healthy foods and survive in a cold world. Later explorers and settlers responded with lethal animosity to large carnivores. Why do those who identify as "real" Westerners harbor attitudes and promote actions hostile to the survival of America's most iconic carnivore, relegating them to token status in the parks of the mountainous West?

10

A Thumb River Bear Charge

From the shore of cold Thumb Lake on Kodiak Island, we watched our air taxi, a Beaver floatplane, depart. The roar of its massive radial engine trailed off in the distance as the plane arced around a distant mountain. Being abandoned to solitude suited us. Pawprints at the water's edge sharpened our anticipation of bears appearing on the nearby river.

I was accompanied by two students, Danielle Chi, who was pursuing her PhD after completing a master's degree on cheetah behavior in California, and Carey Hendrix, a wildlife student, avid hunter, and keen outdoorsman. We had been dropped beside a small cabin, newly built by a native corporation. On discovering its door was unlocked, we defaulted to a tent site nearby. The reality of being on the ground in new, strange grizzly country had begun to sink in. This was no ecotourism hotspot, where every bear had years of close contact with people. The Kodiak bears were heavily hunted, suggesting they would either run when confronted with the sight or smell of humans or charge. Caution was front and center in my mind. However, in our haste to unload the plane and get the pilot on his way, we had failed to check the float compartments, where all of our bear spray and stove fuel were stored.

Thumb River was just a short way down a bear trail from our cabin, where the river emptied into Karluk Lake at the west end of Kodiak Island. The river abounded with salmon and bears but not anglers, photographers, or tour operators. We went to survey it as a potential location for Danielle's project.

As we moved our gear from the lake's edge into the cabin, a good-sized brownie sauntered along the beach. To alert her to our presence, I called out from the porch. "Hey, bear!", not wanting to start our trip with a surprised and upset bear. All was going swimmingly until the bear diverted up the trail toward the cabin. At the same time, I realized I had not brought the shotgun up from the last pile of bags on the shore. Serious oops! We could have retreated inside the cabin, but I knew a bear could pull the door off, if it chose to do so. Instead I went the bluff route and stomped on the wooden floor while telling the bear in a loud voice that it was not invited to the party and ought to get on with its routine. The bear's demeanor suggested that curiosity was driving its approach. The commotion that I created turned it back just as it got to a small shack nearby, where our food was stored. Much relieved, we watched her reverse back down the beach.

We tallied another lesson with that bear: that it is best to be prepared with bear spray and other back-up at *all* times. Keeping calm enough to assess a bear's intentions or motivation is crucial. Regrettably, too many inexperienced hunters have misinterpreted a bear's approach near camp and fired a shot before attempting to shoo the bear away. I understand the anxiety of a group of hunters not wanting to bed down with a persistent grizzly circling camp, but pulling up camp or staying awake with a fire going are still options. Crying "defense of life and property" with an attack story to boot is too often the excuse for what amounts to unnecessary killing a non-threatening bear.

If I had to describe a confrontation with a bear that flooded me with adrenaline in my twenty-five years with bears since being mauled, I would nominate the female with cubs that we encountered the next day.

Early in the morning, enjoying clear weather, we hiked a bear trail next to our cabin through shoulder-high grass to the lip of a steep, muddy cut bank overlooking a curve of the river with ideal visibility along the stream. We saw salmon in the knee-deep water but no bears. Danielle and Carey decided to drop down to the river while I stayed as lookout. I had been down the bluff, but I was so edgy due to the thick vegetation that I hiked back up to the overview. Good thing I did. On a forest trail across the stream, I saw flashes of fur and then two cubs following their mom right to the river, where my students were standing unaware.

The female had not seen any of us yet, but she was closing in quickly. I anticipated serious trouble but did not want to yell for fear of triggering a charge. I caught Danielle's eye and waved frantically for her to come. At the same time, I displayed ten finger "claws," our sign for a bear nearby. Danielle responded in high gear, her petite frame scrambling athletically up the bank. Carey, on the other hand, pulled a camera from his pack and started taking photos. The mother bear entered the water and paced back and forth, the hair bristling on her hump. I had never seen a female so aroused. To me, she telegraphed that she was seconds away from a charge.

Carey persisted in taking pictures despite the bear's threats and my demands to move away. She lunged forward. Carey finally caught up with Danielle and me as we backed swiftly away from the top of the cut bank, anticipating a charge at any moment.

Just as I left the bluff's edge, I saw the angry mom launch a flat-out charge across the river in long leaps, as if there was no water there. In seconds she was on our shore, huffing. On the high bank, both students ran past me and back down the trail while I stayed, preparing for the female's charge over the steep bank. Steep or not, I knew she could climb it in seconds.

As the students disappeared into the five-foot-tall grass, I turned around and bear sprayed a line across the trail, where the bear would come if she broached the lip of the bank. A yellow cloud hissed from the bear spray can, fogging the tunnel-like path in grass so dense and tall that Sumatran tigers might feel at home. I could have used a tall perch about then, but my short-barreled shotgun would have to be my elephant gun. I chambered a shell and prepared to meet the angry bear. Shooting her was the last thing I wanted to do, because it might just be a bluff charge. More significantly, I considered a wounded bear my worst nightmare.

To my surprise, I felt composed and steeled for action. "Don't go Christian on this bear if it crests that cut bank," I muttered to myself. The thought of killing a bear distressed me, but I had vowed not to donate any more tissue to another bear, not that day and not ever.

No bear appeared. She aborted her charge before getting to the lip of the bank. A wave of relief washed over me, but my heart rate took an hour to settle from the adrenaline surge that lubricated a fight-or-flight response. Our mood improved back at the cabin, where a surprise visit from two cinematographers greeted us. They had seen our plane come in and motored over from a refuge cabin on a big island in Karluk Lake. Not only was it reassuring to have some company, they gave us fuel and resupplied us with bear spray from their cache.

We completed our assessment of the site and decided to look elsewhere, as the bear and salmon season there was too short. The close-on charge had provided a demonstration of defensive behavior of a female with cubs in a surprise encounter. The take-home message for me was the texture of the build-up of aggressive signals that she transmitted before launching a full-on charge. It could have been a bluff charge, but we did not stay around long enough to find out.

11

Do Bears Self-Medicate?

You might think few real surprises remained after decades of spying on salmon stream bears. Even less anticipated are observations that make one re-think the cognitive status of bears in general. However, one event was exciting and anomalous, because it suggested some advanced planning by a bear for a specific purpose. Claiming purpose and planning in any animal puts me on thin ice, even thinner ice than uttering anthropomorphisms for the philosophically inclined, but I plead for tolerance, if not acceptance.

In July 2010, I was standing on an elevated platform that overlooked the lower Brooks River and its reedy estuary. A fluffy-eared adult bear waded downstream directly toward me. She hesitated below the viewing platform, dug her heavy-duty claws into the bottom, and lifted a gob of muck to her mouth. I was stunned at her intentional crossing of the river directly to scoop up sediment settled out in a back eddy. As soon as she left, I gouged up a sample. It felt like gritty toothpaste between my fingers. In color and texture, it matched the volcanic ash layered along the road cuts nearby. Later I collected samples from the road to compare the chemical similarity to see why a bear would eat the stuff.

After the female went upstream, I waited for a repeat performance, armed this time with a video camera. Bingo! The same female came along the opposite bank and again diverted across the river to the silty pool. I recorded her dipping a paw and eating a half-cup of mushy ash. This bear definitely included volcanic ash in her diet. I decided to send a sample off for chemical analysis.

A soil scientist in Toronto was interested. He had published papers on chimpanzees eating soil. His tests included chemical composition and examination under a high-powered microscope to look for additional material of possible food value. Chemical analysis showed the mush to be pure silicon dioxide—essentially ground glass. Tiny amounts of algae were present but nothing of food value. If the bear sought out this material, I assumed it must have some health benefit. Humans and many other animals eat clay or dirt, so maybe I could find an answer in those studies. Herbivores eat soil for its mineral content, mainly potassium, to balance all the sodium in their diet. But the ash in water could have no soluble salts remaining. Besides, bears have no craving for salt, given their diverse diet.

Parrots and apes eat clay to remove toxins from unripe fruit or seeds containing bitter or lethal alkaloids. Fine clay particles adsorb or attach to these toxins, which are then excreted, making the plant safe to eat. Since volcanic ash is crystalline, unlike clay, it would not adsorb toxins. Moreover, volcanic ash has nothing in common with bentonite clay, a complex material with different absorptive and adsorptive properties.

These bears eat only salmon and berries, which have no toxins. Another reason for animals and people to eat clay or soil is for essential elements, like phosphorus or iron, otherwise missing in their diet. However, this ash would have nothing for an animal to dissolve and digest in its stomach, because it had been thoroughly rinsed in fresh water. Toxin removal benefits could be ruled out.

Could ash rid a bear of gut parasites? Large volumes of tapeworms occur in bear scats near Brooks River, and other parasites are found in bear intestines. Tapeworms absorb their nutrients from intestinal contents as they hang by a circle of hooks. Maybe the ash could abrade the surface tissue of parasites, causing them to lose fluids. Or perhaps ash particles would jam up the mouth parts of nematodes. Experiments with diatomaceous earth have been effective in ridding caged pigeons of gut nematodes, giving support to the self-medication idea, although the way it works is unknown.

Dr. Michael Huffman of the Primate Research Institute of Kyoto University has observed chimpanzees partially chew and swallow wads of leaves of African plants, which caused the animals to expel masses of parasites in their feces. This was done by sick or listless animals, qualifying it as self-medication.

Brooks bears also self-medicated by eating coarse grass and swallowing it without much chewing. I only saw this in fall, when grass is woody and low in nutrients. Plugs of grass going through a bear's gut would scrape off attached tapeworms, a process I called the "Brillo pad" effect. Grass and piles of tapeworms occurred in bear scats in the fall. If a bear's intestine contained many worms, then the worms would compete for the bear's nutrients. Large numbers of tapeworms holding on to the intestine might also block the passage and absorption of salmon.

Dr. John Holmes, a parasitologist in biological sciences at the University of Alberta, has noted large boluses of undigested grass and tapeworms in snow geese dung. After eating grass, their mid-lower guts were found to be completely clean, with no tapeworms attached. In both bears and geese, tapeworms were shed around a time of critical nutritional stress. Clearing the gut of parasites may be especially significant for an animal entering a den for half a year.

Medicine Bears

If bears can treat their own diseases, how was this learned? Laboratory rats are capable of selecting the healthier of two diets, avoiding ones lacking an essential amino acid, for example. This means they can link a beneficial outcome (nutritional satisfaction) with taste cues. This is the reverse of taste-aversion conditioning, where stomach illness is associated with a novel flavor, leading to rejection of that flavor. Bears could be learning to rid themselves of parasites by sensing good outcomes, maybe less intestinal pain.

Self-medication could be passed on to cubs, when they have opportunities for observational learning while following their mother in the first two or three years of life. This social learning involves observing the mother's behavior and locations and repeating them later when solitary. The solitary nature of bears is greatly exaggerated: not only is there a close bond with the mother, siblings or companions form associations after they separate from their mother. Pair bonds can be protective against other bears and also provide an opportunity to exchange behavior patterns, which are learned through observation. In a later chapter, I explain that this is how grizzly bears learn to avoid being shot, since a companion may have been wounded or killed, and the survivor makes the association between humans and injury, leading to avoidance of people.

Then there is the question of how these habits begin. It is known that foods that make animals sick cause post-ingestive conditioning, and the animals avoid the smell or taste of those foods when encountered again. We used lithium chloride salt on black bears in our field tests to inhibit bears from breaking into bee yards, with some success. The bears associated the stomach illness caused by tasteless LiCl (enclosed in watertight packets) with the taste of honey and bee brood and subsequently avoided these foods. Their digestive and nervous system is built to connect any food, especially new ones, with later stomach upset.

When animals consume soil to provide missing elements, it is labeled nutritional wisdom, a bit of a grandiose term for learning what makes it feel good or bad. For the feeding on inert ash, we can only assume that a bear senses an improvement of some kind. Otherwise, I remain baffled by the behavior.

Aircraft prepares to drop smoke-jumper/EMT crew and medical pack for Crowfoot Ridge rescue, Yellowstone National Park

Brooks River brown bears feasting on salmon

Surplus of salmon carcasses at the end of the summer spawning season

Bear chases after salmon on southwest Alaska's coast

National Park Service

Airplanes block bear's path so she swims around them with her cub

Field observer in elevated stand testing paint-ball gun

One of three bear-viewing platforms at Brooks River Katmai National Park, Alaska

Michelle McLellan

This adult female turned away when yelled at from a nearby platform

Anthony Crupi

Brooks River bear eating volcanic ash scooped from river bottom

Shea Wyatt

Cubs learning to find fish in Glendale River, Knight Inlet, BC

Young black bear seeking refuge from other bears at Anan Creek, SE Alaska

Historical photo of visitors viewing bears at a Sequoia National Park incinerator

Owen Nevin

Adult male bear scent marking a tree on the British Columbia coast

Katmai brown bear after a season of eating Brooks River salmon

Young bear tolerates close approach at Geographic Harbor, Katmai National Park

Shea Wyatt

Female with two cubs fishing at Knight Inlet, British Columbia

PART 3

Bears in Ecosystems: Essential Links Through Evolution

12

Salmon Bears Build Rainforests

A Keystone Species for Bears, Forests, and Oceans

Growing up on the shore of Lake Ontario, I was always in the water, diving into my fantasies as Jacques Cousteau. Fish were perfect little creatures, especially schools of transparent pinhead minnows, which I netted. As an undergraduate in biology, I wrote my first term paper on the life cycle of salmon, enthralled by their ability to navigate home from distant seas and arrive at the same stream in which they had hatched.

As a graduate student at Duke University, I caught the ecology wave as it rolled into the zoology curriculum. Ecosystems, energy flow, and atoms of carbon, nitrogen, and phosphorus cycling around made my mind race. The role of salmon in fertilizing lakes, rivers, and upslope to mountain landscapes fit right in. This was *the* big new idea. Think never-ending schools of fish transferring nitrogen and phosphorus from the sea to terrestrial systems, generously fertilizing giant coastal Sitka spruce and Western hemlock. This magical process counteracted the constant leaching of soil nutrients by rain and gravity, draining soil vitals off to sea. After spawning salmon die, they decompose to fertilize plankton blooms in lakes, which feed the salmon's young. Surely this gift from the gods would not be degraded—until it was. Various mega-dams, over-harvesting through commercial fishing, agriculture, and massive clear-cutting ground up spawning habitat. Like much industrial momentum, these monstrous monuments to engineering soldiered blindly onward, well ahead of any ecological understanding or appreciation of the ecosystem produced by salmon in the watersheds of the Columbia, Fraser, Stikine, and the Naknek river stewards. Gradually, a cottage industry of scientists initiated projects on the benefits of salmon that went beyond fertilizing lakes to the salmon's key role in building coastal forest biodiversity and ramping up productivity.

Salmon are fuel for bears and fertilizer for the entire Katmai ecosystem, from streams to shrubby mountain slopes and forests. Katmai, buried in volcanic ash in the 1912 Novarupta explosion, rebloomed, phoenix-like, to grow richer with more niches, more species, and more routes for energy and nutrients to flow through the landscape's food webs. Maybe this "bear factory" started small, like a little automobile assembly shop. Then, with inputs of energy and material, native tribes watched the little buggy shop transform into the world's biggest assembly line for mass-produced bears and biodiversity. Just like an auto factory would fail if electricity and steel supplies were restricted, so too would this natural system decline if the salmon were choked off. The vast Pacific was the supply chain for self-propelled salmon, which flooded into networks of streams in the towering Aleutian Range of the Alaska Peninsula. This abundance of ocean riches infused life into the otherwise barren landscape and annually stoked terrestrial life's fires. So abundant were these mobile, finny fat packs that all manner of meat eaters, especially bears, came and grew so fat so fast that they put a smiley face on obesity. Only as overweight animals could they have survived the inner-space voyage of a winter den. Those bears that memorized the precise routes to each dining site and were prompt enough to overcome the competition ascended the evolutionary ladder.

Grizzly Bears Transport of Salmon Nutrients at Landscape Scales

We should back up and mentally re-calibrate for time scales in millennia, when unimaginable numbers of salmon returned yearly from the open ocean of Pacific Northwest waters to spawn and die throughout coastal watersheds. Biologists struggled to grasp the immensity and significance of this natural subsidy of fertilizer and energy being transferred upslope to forests, streams, and people on the coast. It was an input of ocean nutrients that any forester or farmer could only dream about. Nowhere else have species like salmon combed the oceans, grown mature, then returned inland like tidal waves as they raced up rivers and streams. Over twenty-two species of vertebrates transported fish nutrients, often in pieces, into riparian zones and old-growth forests. My colleague at Utah State University, Dr. James Long, explained to me how essential this fertilizing service is to the growth rates of Herculean coastal forests, which have exceeded the growth rates of tropical rainforests.

Now people know why all the coastal rivers did not wash out all the nutrients and leave deserts in the high country. Thank you, salmon. Even when the land was scoured by ice sheets or blasted barren by volcanic eruptions, these fish restored fertility to the land. Eventually, towering forests developed, where the temperature, soil, and rainfall were optimal. The bears, aboriginal peoples, and other salmon chasers did their part in preparing the soil for the seeds of berries they had eaten along their trails.

On any trip to Pacific coastal estuaries, visitors have witnessed where salmon have sustained marine life and terrestrial predators and scavengers, such as wolves, eagles, and gulls. Human subsistence fit in here too, except when rapacious exploitation became industrial in scale. Space-age technology and machinery drove many biological factories into bankruptcy. Exporting salmon yanked a piece out of the loop, because the nutrients were shipped elsewhere. Woe to the short-sighted culture that broke this sacred offering.

Grizzly bears, because of their size and mobility, moved fertilizers to forests over longer distances than smaller animals, like river otters, and distributed more enriching nitrates and phosphates in the form of feces, urine, and fish parts. In 2001, over seventy Katmai bears came to Brooks River and fed on one population of sockeye salmon (*Onchorhynchus nerka*) over a four-month period, as described earlier.

Katmai's coastal grizzlies, captured and collared for population assessment after the Exxon-Valdez oil spill, proved to be the densest population of grizzlies ever measured—550 bears per 1,000 square kilometers. We knew these roaming bears distributed fertilizer over vast areas, but how could the ecological impact be measured? A student from Utah State University, Arthur Morris, measured stable nitrogen isotopes, a nutrient of marine origin, in soil along BC's bear trails. He showed conclusively that soil near the trails contained much more marine-derived material than similar areas away from bear trails.

Where bears learned to access abundant salmon efficiently, their numbers peaked, approaching the maximum growth possible in terms of stature and number of offspring. This successful foraging behavior has parallels with increased biodiversity in the entire ecosystem, as first demonstrated in studies of water chemistry in Karluk Lake and Kodiak Island. In the 1930s, Chauncey Juday, a Yale University lake specialist, discovered how essential salmon carcasses were to the growth of the plankton that young salmon feed on in nursery lakes. By the 1990s, teams of researchers focused on how important salmon nutrients were to the growth of riparian and upland vegetation, especially trees like giant Sitka spruce, which reached maximum size near salmon streams. The concept of salmon in the trees was born.

Conveyer Belts: Salmon to Bears to Forests

In July 1991, while I waited in my tree platform for bear activity, I wondered what effect superabundant salmon had on bear density in Katmai. Years later, an answer came from a synthesis of the most reliable population studies of grizzly bears in Alaska by Dr. Sterling Miller and his colleagues. Their conclusions were that bear populations that depended largely on salmon were over a hundred times as dense as those without salmon, a relationship confirmed later.

In coastal Alaska, bears acquire more than 90 percent of their food from marine sources, mainly salmon but also clams, mussels, and crabs, when salmon are not running. This dependence of coastal grizzly bears on marine animals has been verified through nitrogen isotope analysis. We consider these coastal grizzlies to be marine bears, like the polar bear. The essential linkage of bear density to salmon availability is accentuated further by the overlap between the seasonal super abundance of salmon and the gluttonous consumption required of bears before entering dens.

The Great Bear Rainforest

In 1995, I sailed into the Great Bear Rainforest with Round River Conservation to help map grizzly bear trail locations and signs of their presence. With their director, Denis Sizemore, we motored by inflatable boat up frigid rivers, then hiked muddy bear trails following streams into the temperate rainforests of northwestern BC. River valleys there have deep, rich soils and giant trees supporting a fertile complex ecosystem, not unlike the Great Barrier Reef. The forests are luxurious in abundance but less diverse in species than tropical rainforests. At one time, its bear population was among the densest in the world. The combination of moderate temperatures and high rainfall year-round (hyper-maritime in geographer jargon) and alluvial soils enriched by salmon and plant litter provide optimal growing conditions for titanic trees and abundant animals. I continue to marvel at how time and evolution have assembled this awesome life zone.

One visit became forever infused in my mind. That cool morning, we left our trimaran sailboat and canoed across Namu Lake to a remote headwater stream. After we scrambled ashore, a bear trail led us through the densest mass of virgin old growth I had ever seen—mostly Western Hemlock and Sitka Spruce. I was stunned. This stand of giants reminded me of the Sequoia Groves on the west slope of the Sierra Range. It felt like there was more wood than air in that dank riparian forest. We were surrounded by trees bigger and more crowded than seen in photographs of ancient coastal forests. They had been fertilized for centuries by salmon carcasses brought there by summer bears or carried over the streambanks in floods from autumn storms. The name "Great Bear Rainforest" is fitting, because bears are the ecological lynchpin in these coastal forests. Ian McAllister, an early defender of this land and the leader of our exploration party, popularized the name.

After the last glaciers scoured the continent, trees, salmon, and bears contributed to the staggering growth and diversity of plants and animals. It was a self-organized or bootstrapped system. Each new species added to the cycle of energy and matter, jump-starting the biological factory. The annual flow of salmon was the supply chain of fertilizer for this factory. Fish returning from the Pacific struck far inland and upslope into vast networks of lakes and rivers in BC and Alaska. Salmon are keystone species here, the superstars in the ecological theater, vital for all living things, green and otherwise. Grizzly bears have been the prime transporters of large quantities of salmon tissue, fertilizing vegetation wherever they go. The bears also create vegetation by distributing enormous numbers of berry seeds. Johnny Appleseed has some competition!

The specialization of bears on salmon was foundational for high survival and reproduction of bear populations. Where bears have been protected from hunting, like the McNeil River Sanctuary, about 144 individuals come to the falls to capture salmon. Because fish concentrate at one place and time, grizzlies need protection from harassment or disturbance by people. Any serious decline of salmon, destruction of spawning habitat, or warming of streams (from climate change) will damage this cornucopia for bears and its enjoyment by people.

A similar decline has happened in BC when stream temperatures rose from exposure to sunlight due to clear-cut forests, low rainfall, or climate change. Water temperatures became lethal for fish. Recent droughts have presented early warning of the effects of shallow streams and rising temperatures. Trapped in pools, salmon die from lack of oxygen.

When fish populations collapse, large carnivores, like bears, abandon traditional areas and begin to range widely, often drawn into coastal villages by food odors. When the land can no longer support the same density of animals, they come to our supplies or starve. Both outcomes lead to dead bears and decimated local populations.

Declines in bears and other salmon eaters herald the unraveling of ecosystem integrity—ecosystems that arose on the foundation of salmon. As a large, wide-ranging mammal, the grizzly bear is irreplaceable for distribution of ocean nutrients far into coastal landscapes.

Bootstrapped Ecosystems

Soon after Katmai's volcanoes smothered plant and animal life in ash, food webs rebuilt from the bottom up. But Alaska had an immigrant jump-starter from distant seas, pelagic salmon, returning to complete their cycle. They constituted a self-priming nutrient pump—slow at first, then accelerated as food web complexity and positive feedback from dead salmon mushroomed. The juicy stew from disintegrating salmon flowed into creeks and lakes to grow salmon fry fast.

This process is a crucial ecological service. Initially, bears were thought to simply distribute fish parts, urine, and feces, fertilizing stream-side soil. But far more likely is the value of matter dropped throughout the network of trails up and around lake tributaries, where salmon die after spawning. This larger scale and its implications boggle the imagination. All this complexity is built on fish flesh flooding into streams in astonishing amounts, bringing to mind invasions of sea turtles crawling up a moonlit beach to bury their eggs in the sand.

Could these huge bears have played an even more central role in this eco-theater? Re-cycling, magnified by a positive feedback in the nutrient system, led to ever-increasing layers of biodiversity, as in a tropical rainforest. In Katmai's case, the feedback produced a re-loading effect of annual nutrients accumulated in the living system. Here the same mechanism for upslope enrichment that compensates for erosional loss of important nutrients was the basis of a continuing cycle. So much emphasis has been placed on the degradation of biological productivity and so little on the reverse. Only a few investigators have focused on how simple systems became increasingly complex and more productive.

The abstract idea of accentuated biodiversity through self-organizing processes based on a salmon-bear-forest delivery system points to related issues. How can so many big bears come together so peacefully? The main factor was the exceptional availability of salmon over large areas for long periods of time. But if salmon were abundant at just a few riffles and unavailable elsewhere, the bear population would be more limited. The bears would be smaller in stature and less densely congregated in a small area. The same would be true if salmon were abundant but came later in the summer or fall. But Katmai had salmon early, late, and everywhere, all vulnerable to being caught.

Bears on the Beach

From the Alaskan Peninsula to Vancouver Island, nutrients from ocean upwelling and flowing from coastal streams has created an amazing diversity of marine life. Plankton, carried by strong tidal flow, are captured by sessile creatures on rocks and wood and in sand and mud, all providing a source of foods for foraging bears. On beaches along the Pacific coast of Katmai National Park, the sea supports dozens of species of mollusks. These clams, oysters, and mussels are rich in lipids and fats, similar to salmon in their contribution to bear survival and prolific reproduction.

This rich intertidal life was exploited by another hunter-gatherer, the Paleo-Indians, who came along the ice-free coast of North America about seventeen thousand years ago. From their boats, they would have seen bears digging up mollusks at low tide. The evidence of long use has been found in kitchen middens of these first people near Namu on BC's central coast. Archeologists have excavated massive mounds of shells dating back over ten thousand years.

13

The Rapid Evolution of Bear Behaviour

Any fan of Darwin's study of Galapagos Islands finches and Peter and Rosemary Grant's stunning demonstration of the rapid micro-evolution of beak structure in these birds under severe drought conditions understands that evolutionary change can be quick. We are accustomed to thinking of evolution as a process taking eons to create change toward new species, but the Grants measured distinct changes in a few generations when selection favored robust, seed-cracking bills under near-starvation conditions. If we substitute behavioral variation for beak variation, we have a mechanism for the adaptation of bears to people when food is abundant. In this chapter, I make the case, a speculative one for sure, because the sophisticated and dedicated collection of field data that the Grants analyzed has not been done in this case.

At Brooks Camp, it only took one day among bears to be astonished, mystified, or enthralled by their tolerance of people. Compared to mountain grizzlies, their apparent unconcern with anglers and hikers seemed counter to lore. Could a new bear culture have arisen, like those that occurred in killer whales or chimpanzees? The differences in behavior of Brooks bears and Yellowstone grizzlies is dazzling when acknowledged.

Earlier, I referred to a very different view of the behavior of Brooks bears. Two grizzly bear experts, Chris Servheen and John Schoen, had submitted a letter to the NPS in 1998, saying the interactions of bears with people at Brooks were so dangerous that "it was not a matter of if, but when there would be a serious injury." Since they were invited as consultants with wide experience (and not inclined to generalize or parrot traditional myths), who was right? Neither the park's history of benign human-bear interactions nor a dozen peer-reviewed papers diluted their acidic assessment. What could account for such un-grizzly-like adaptations to people? Managers should decide after a consultation with local and outside experts after the histories that underlie differences in grizzly populations have been considered.

I made dozens of observations of mother bears tolerating people near their cubs. There was no question that these tolerant mothers behaved differently when a large adult male approached. Alaskan bears have lived for millennia near aboriginal people, who mostly tolerated bears when harvesting salmon. They accommodated them, feared them, and/or worshipped them but rarely hunted these "ferocious" creatures. The bears, it seems, treat people more tolerantly than they treat their own kind. Indeed, rangers at Brooks frequently explained to visitors that these bears are wary of other bears, not so much of us. All the behavioral studies confirmed that bears continued to grow more habituated to the upright apes, even if they operated noisy machines.

Over the millennia since the last ice sheet retreated, Brooks River has had bears with ready access to salmon at the falls and in shallow streams. These bears, predisposed genetically to minimize fighting and maximize catching time, have thrived, as Mr. Darwin suggested. Competition that risks injury and interferes with hunting fish is a failed strategy in evolutionary terms. I conclude that their relative tolerance of other bears transfers to people as well, since bears pretty much ignore them.

Each new generation of cubs came to this human-dominated habitat and learned that salmon and harmless hominids go together. What other conditions could explain the rapid development of tolerance? First, salmon streams, crowded with bears for centuries, promoted unusual bear-to-bear tolerance. What may have begun as an individual trait was incorporated genetically as a behavioral predisposition for tolerance. Alternatively, the Brooks River regulars were that segment of the regional population that accepted the hassle that came with fishing among lots of bears and people. Maximizing food intake and minimizing competition and injury was adaptive under conditions of food surplus, but it was not in the playbook for grizzlies in Rocky Mountain habitats. Maximizing food intake and minimizing competition and injury was adaptive where food was overflowing, but this was never the case for grizzles in the Rocky Mountains. One exception may have been in Yellowstone in the early 1970s, when dozens of grizzlies fed close together in the massive garbage dumps, a situation that the Craighead brothers called eco-centers, comparing them to salmon streams. Interestingly, this aggregation of grizzlies around garbage had one hundred years of history, supporting the concept of a novel culture, artificial though it was.

Impoverished habitat set the stage for intolerance between bears, because territorial defense paid off. Grizzlies became more competitive and intolerant of each other when food stressed. That intolerance likely carried over to interactions with people—which were frequently unpleasant. Adding to the crankiness brought on by hunger, mountain bears received punishment from human contact, including wounds or threats when approaching hunting camps or livestock. Problem bears, trained in crime, have become victims when transported to unfamiliar territory, where finding food and avoiding resident bears aggravates their stress. For research grizzlies in the Yellowstone ecosystem, being captured and collared equated to thirty-five years of abusive handling of hundreds of bears.

A look back into the history of Yellowstone's grizzlies revealed cultural residue or a hang-over of early mistreatment. Fear and wariness are passed on by those with memories from escapes of the prolonged culling of over 223 grizzlies following the closure of garbage dumps in the 1970s. Yellowstone bears that had been accustomed over generations to feeding on thousands of pounds of food dumped from hotels and campgrounds suddenly switched to fresher "garbage" in campgrounds when the dumps were closed. Park managers decided the bears should go "cold turkey" when dumps were closed precipitously. Bear managers were sure the bears would go back to natural food, a notion conceived in ignorance and the opposite of what grizzly bear experts predicted. When bears entered campgrounds, as the Craigheads predicted, they were viewed as threats, and rangers were ordered to shoot, shovel, and shut up. The only cover-up took place in head office.

My experience in Yellowstone with grizzlies and then with black bears in Yosemite left me thinking that co-existence with bears among throngs of park visitors had a long road ahead for success, if it was even possible. This conclusion soon collided with reality when I arrived in Katmai, where bears in large numbers wandered among people in equally large numbers along trails and among anglers wading and casting for rainbow trout and salmon. The crucial difference in Brooks bears that explained their adaptation to people rested on some combination of natural surplus foods (salmon and berries), no food conditioning, and no capture, handling, or aversive training, except for the odd juvenile needing a bit of tough love to shape up his behavior.

It took time and comparisons across bear-viewing sites to untangle the impressive differences in the aggressive behavior of grizzlies toward humans in national parks, especially how the bears' reactions depended on our treatment of them. The most tolerant bears had learned from frequent contacts with humans that no harm ensued. The best examples were in large national parks, like Katmai, where bears were protected for generations from all kinds of lethal interactions, especially hunting.

The same conditions existed for the bears at McNeil Falls, which were protected in a state refuge decades earlier.

Animals with large brains have made behavioral changes based on observation of other bears when finding food, escaping predators, and obtaining mates. This established a cultural tradition after it spread among the group. If the learned pattern was sufficiently beneficial, these individuals grew faster, survived longer, and outbred those that did not. As a consequence, the underlying genetic facilitators for the learned behavior became established in the population. The rate of micro-evolution depended on the amount of variation in the gene pool and the degree of genetic control. Over time, the specific pattern of behavior was displayed in all members of the population and became what some called instinctive or wired-in behavior. Wariness toward people or any new situation was said to be a characteristic of the population. This process was first proposed by J. M. Baldwin in 1887 (known as the Baldwin Effect), an early stage in evolutionary change. In fact, it accounts for much cultural variation in animals, such as the divergence in behavior after the appearance of powerful selective forces, such as the removal of animals with modern firearms.

After I applied the Baldwin effect to bear behavior when I came to Katmai, I was pleased to find that the late Norwegian scientist, Kare Elgmork, had also described cryptic or retiring behavior in a population of brown bears in 1987. He attributed their shyness to bear hunting. Ernest Thompson Seton, to my surprise, long ago speculated about the same effect in a chapter in *Lives of Game Animals Vol. II,* entitled "Alaskan Giant Brown-Bear."

> The giant has become inoffensive now. He is shy, indeed, and seeks only to be let mind his own business. At the slightest hint of man in his vicinity, he will fly fast and far, and covers many mountains to be sure that he has left the dreaded taint behind. It is modern guns that has made this change of heart.

Changes in behavior toward humans goes beyond the individual's memory of traumatic or frightening events, even appearing generations later. Offspring observe their mother's alarmed behavior, identify the cause of the alarm, and mirror her response. This social transmission of fear response has been documented with other birds and mammals. There is no reason to assume bears cannot do the same.

Many wildlife biologists resist the idea that bears learn anything from being hunted. A common argument is that the target animal is dead, so there is no opportunity to learn. An entire book could be devoted to mechanisms of transmission of risk awareness in animals, but the essential fact, often missed, is that most animals survive after being targeted or wounded by shooters and learn from the experience.

A dramatic and instructive example of cultural transmission in animals came from an attempt to cull elephants in South Africa almost one hundred years ago. According to lifelong elephant expert Ian Douglas-Hamilton, about 140 elephants had been raiding citrus crops, doing constant damage. This led to a plan to annihilate them all. Rather than swift destruction of the herd, a marksman was chosen who, unfortunately, preferred to kill one animal at a time using a rifle. Members of the herd observed others dying before they escaped into the forest. After a year, the thirty or fewer survivors became extremely wary and only left the forest after dark. This behavior continued over many years despite no further killing or harassment. Ultimately, a sanctuary was established for the population. Even in 1975, Douglas-Hamilton reported that the herds were still nocturnal and extremely aggressive toward people, despite the fact that no elephants that had witnessed the culling remained alive. He attributed this to the fear responses of mothers toward humans being transmitted to their calves over several generations. Although this does not mean a genetic awareness or fear of humans had evolved, it shows how fear responses can be socially transmitted. If some equally powerful type of selection for wary behavior were to continue, it would be reasonable to expect that a more skittish phenotype or visible characteristic might have become genetically incorporated.

Large-brained mammals, such as dolphins, elephants, and grizzly bears, are capable of rapid behavioral change or cultural evolution, because learned skills are programmed into every generation. Reflecting on my personal experience with the Yellowstone grizzly, I wanted to know if capturing grizzlies shortened their fuse in encounters with people on trails. I know of two incidents of grizzlies killing people shortly after the bears recovered from anesthetic. What a bear learns from being trapped or drugged depends on the intensity of psychological stress and pain experienced during the process.

On the other hand, the black bears in Yosemite that I knew about, habituated to people and food conditioned from generations of campers, became larger on average, raised more offspring, and the larger males dominated breeding. Given enough time, this was a successful formula for the evolution of a new subspecies—*Ursus followus*. Other bears that avoided people and fed naturally were outcompeted, or females mated with larger, dominant males. Their offspring drifted genetically toward the newer adaptive state. When these changes were tolerated by managers, bear conflicts and property damage increased dramatically, because a behavioral epidemic was spreading among the bears. The next challenge—documented so well by ranger Rachel Mazur in Yosemite—was a period of window smashing of parked cars, another innovation that was only halted when the perpetrators were euthanized. So ended that cultural revolution!

Sooner or later, park managers will recognize that they face conflicting objectives: accommodating hordes of naïve (and a few misbehaving) visitors in Sierra campgrounds while attempting to maintain a natural population of black bears. Habituated bears have continued to investigate potential foods unless their security is so interrupted that they revert to natural foods, like the Rocky Mountain National Park bears. Alternatively, they are eliminated, like the California grizzly bear was years ago. Another strategy has worked if given adequate resources of people and funds. Biologists have collared problem bears and tracked them just prior to entering campgrounds. Such intensive management has been successful so far, but the ethics and pragmatic assessment remains open.

If we wish to have bears to co-exist with, then more restraint and less aggressive dominance of wildlife is needed from humans. The public's love affair with Yellowstone tells us that our society needs more wilderness for wild animals.

14

Calculating Bears

Daycare for Cubs

On the lower Brooks River, Arctic terns filled the air with raspy screams as they circled tightly and dove for salmon eggs, little orange balls tumbling along the river gravel. Farther down river, I saw a female bear park her cubs at the end of the floating bridge and leave—an odd choice right next to one of the busiest paths at Brooks Camp. With her cubs settled in beside the trail, a ranger marched up, intent on holding back visitors about to crowd the cubs. Was this a bad mom who had abandoned her cubs or a brilliant plan for child care?

Watching this scenario break out from across the river in early September gave me new insights into grizzly intelligence. It reminded me of the calm mother I mentioned earlier, diving for fish out in the lake, who gave only a passing glance my way when her cubs approached me along the Naknek Lake edge. In both cases, the relaxed mom carried on, seeing only people near her cubs. Naturalist, author, and filmmaker Charlie Russell called this babysitting behavior. It says a lot about a grizzly's ability to connect complicated events and relationships, especially relative to the dispute over whether hunting bears make them avoid people. Being able to teach a truant bear to avoid people could save it from being destroyed. So, what did that mom have in mind when she deposited the kids near a crowd?

Usually, female bears with alley-cat-sized cubs are intensely protective, keeping them within a few feet. Any squawk from a cub brings an instant alert and action from momma. The biggest threats for a female with new cubs at a salmon stream are large adult males, who sometimes kill cubs. However, on salmon streams with anglers and photographers, the adult males usually stay away. They can be seen if you come quietly at dawn but soon disappear if they sense human presence. This avoidance of people by males appears to be understood by females. In effect, people present a shield for bears with cubs, somewhat like a tree for the cubs to climb, permitting mom to go off to fish, knowing her cubs are safe. For a while, some newer seasonal rangers at Brooks were convinced this bear was a "bad" mom, because she abandoned her cubs. However, she just delegated the job to rangers who, predictably, kept all visitors back or in a circle, waiting for the cubs to move off. They did not move off though, because their mom gave them a signal to stay put. So, the cubs wrestled or played with their toes until their mother returned. Visitors being held up might seem a trivial inconvenience, until the need for people to catch their planes to make connections to Anchorage for flights to London, Sweden, or Japan becomes imminent.

When I grasped the mom's ploy, I convinced the rangers to violate the fifty-yard rule and quietly guide a few people at a time past the lolling cubs. It was not a permanent solution, because it had the disadvantage of confusing the public with a message that distance rules could be broken.

The mental gymnastics for a bear to make all the connections in this picture looked Einsteinian, because mother bear had linked three insights: the threat of predatory male bears, an awareness of male bears' avoidance of humans and predictably benign humans. She recognized an opportunity to place her cubs in a secure location. Alternatively, her tactic might simply be a narrowing of her responses to a threat from males after seeing no threats from people: a learned pattern. In other words, she learned that being near people meant not having adult males around. Either way, it was an example of the degree to which grizzlies cognitively connect situations in their environment, a capacity that can be used for protection and conservation of bears.

What Do Bears Learn from Being Hunted?

If you want to start a minor riot among bear biologists or hunters, ask if hunting bears makes them avoid people. The issue is deceptively complex. Some think a truism will do—a dead bear cannot learn anything. True, but all bullets fired do not kill. Therefore, we need to ask if a wounded bear learns something. No doubt! What if a companion has been wounded or killed? Another yes. How about if alone and shot at? That depends, but likely the bear will associate events, especially if it has encountered hunters previously. I have caused nearby bears to run off by working the pump action of a shotgun, which created a harsh metal-on-metal sound as I jacked a shell into the gun's chamber. The noise was unlike any other sound in nature and worked well for announcing human presence. Also, it may have had special meaning for a bear that had been shot at or wounded, not too different from your dog recognizing your jangling car keys and realizing an outing is at hand.

Experiences at many bear-viewing sites, along with reports from other observers, demonstrate that hunting has kept large adult male bears away from people at bear-viewing areas. Reliable support for this comes from observational studies at Karluk Lake viewing areas on Kodiak Island, Alaska, and Knight Inlet Lodge near the Glendale River, BC. A 1989–1991 study in BC of seven radio-collared adult male grizzlies in the Khutzeymateen Valley concluded that most left the valley after the first year. Circumstantial evidence suggests that prior years of bear hunting in the drainage and the capturing effects caused those males to abandon the habitat. However, thirteen females, some with young, continued feeding in the study area, where they had been collared.

Adult males get to grow old and large by becoming nocturnal, to avoid people. But this is not the same as saying that grizzlies "need to be hunted to teach them to respect people." As an aversive training tactic, hunting fails, because truant bears may not be the ones conditioned, only the bears behaving naturally. This is far too blunt an instrument for preventing damage or injuries to people. Besides, if so many grizzlies were shot at to make them avoid all human contact, the degree of negative impacts on bears would almost defy description. We know the effects of harassment and punishment.

Bear managers in Alaska promoted the slogan "a fed bear is a dead bear" to alert people to the detrimental effects of garbage and other foods accessible to bears. Far less attention has been paid to the consequences of chronic punishment. By avoiding humans instead of finding food, bears have been displaced from secure areas that have preferred foods. Chronically harassed bears that abandon good habitat for less-productive ones become smaller and have fewer cubs. In an earlier chapter, I explained the experience of biologist Hank McCutchen. The sub-group of bears living at 9,000–11.000 feet were tiny—females averaged 120 pounds and males 175 pounds. The ecology and behavior of these bears was changed detrimentally due to four underlying causes. Initially, fire suppression inside the park degraded bear habitat by leaving a more mature forest with less food. Second, these bears avoided people on trails in the better habitat along streams, lowering the carrying capacity for bears. Third, outside the park, urban development had fragmented and usurped bear habitat. Finally, legal hunting was intensive, and males especially were being killed. All this knock-on damage by humans on a small population created what McCutchen called cryptic bears, a good term for the behavioral syndrome, because the bears became almost invisible.

Observational Learning by Social Bears

Circling back to the question of how hunting affects bears, we needed to know how fear responses are transmitted in bears. We have already considered the case of one member of a pair being injured or killed and the survivor making the association. Also, shy mothers signal alarm that is detected by her cubs. The cubs connect or associate any unusual event in the environment that accompanies the alarm and retreat. Lesson learned.

Many shots fired by hunters are misses or wound the animal slightly. A study by Arizona wildlife biologists gives some intriguing insights. They placed a mounted deer along a road to investigate deer poaching. The results were dramatic. From a hidden site, the biologists watched and later determined that one third of the shots at the stuffed, motionless deer were kills, one third were considered to wound the animal, such that it might survive, and the last third were complete misses! If the target were a moving grizzly bear, it seems likely that a hunter would fire even more erratically, perhaps due to "buck fever" or the looming fear of the reaction of a wounded grizzly. Grizzlies can survive major wounds, at least for a while, so the wounded-and-recovered explanation seems credible. When hunters prize larger male bears as trophies, pressure is concentrated on fewer individual bears. This contributes to avoidance of humans by males where hunting efforts have been intense.

Other types of punishing run-ins with humans include snaring and culvert trapping by research biologists. In these operations, the captured grizzly was undoubtedly very unhappy, biting and clawing at whatever it could to escape. When a biologist approached to immobilize the bear, it had every opportunity to see, smell, or hear the source of its misfortune. Lots of learning going on there. These darting operations generated frantic escape attempts, as the psychological and physical punishment was not dissimilar to harassment. The point here is not to assign blame but to ask what impacts on a bear's attitudes or personality have resulted from such interactions. We know that some bears seemed unfazed, returning to be trapped again, presumably for the food rewards. Biologists call these bears "trap happy." Unfortunately, we have no good science that explains how handled bears relate to people on trails later. One federal research project in the Greater Yellowstone ecosystem assessed the behavioral reaction of collared bears to being approached by a person. There is one remarkable account of a veteran grizzly who, after being trapped and collared twenty-three times, kept a biologist up a tree for much of a long night. I know two people who have been killed by bears recovering from immobilization, but this hardly permits us to generalize about the effect on other bears. However, the large number of people hiking in grizzly country demands better information about the likelihood of grizzlies developing aggressive attitudes toward people after being handled.

Grizzly bears are more social than the label "solitary" implies. While they are not pack animals, like wolves and lions, the relationship between a cub and its mother is relatively long, typically three years, and quite intense. Cubs are among the smallest of mammal newborns and vulnerable to many mishaps, making long-term parental care crucial to their survival. A close relationship also fosters endless opportunities for observational learning. One marvelous story came from McNeil River about a young bear that mimicked its mother's fishing technique. The youngster followed its mom into the river and fished from the same rock as she did. It even sat in the same orientation to the river and with the same paw in the air that she did to catch fish.

After cubs leave their mother, they maintain their social longings, often forming coalitions with a sibling or joining another lone two-year-old. To an extent, this substitutes for the bond it had with its mother and improves defense against other bears. Another plus—each member of the pair can observe and learn from the other, especially from threats that could cause injury or death. At this stage, bears explore and innovate, sometimes pushing the limits with humans. When they are rewarded by unsecured foods, such as in campgrounds, the outcome is predictable: recurring damage and a dead bear.

Raiding Seabird Nests

Observational learning has resulted in behavioral traditions among Alaskan grizzlies that almost defy belief. Edgar Bailey, a renowned Alaskan seabird biologist, monitored bird colonies on remote islands in the Shelikof Straits off Katmai's stormy coast for decades. He saw over forty bears, including female bears with cubs, swimming across the open sea to raid seabird nests. His photographs show bears swimming at sea, coming ashore, and pillaging nests of hole-nesting birds. No one knows how these bears became aware of such rich sources of food. One island was over thirty miles from the mainland, so vision was unlikely. Perhaps onshore winds brought the odors of the dense bird colonies to the mainland. Katmai coastal history provides a stunning example of bear discovery and solidification of bear culture.

Sagas of swimming bears being speared from boats were told by indigenous coastal villagers. Within modern times, this hunting tradition died out, perhaps because so many bears died that way. Grizzlies were defenseless and acutely vulnerable when swimming. Then Novarupta volcano exploded in 1912, burying villages along the Alaskan Peninsula, which forced abandonment by survivors. This ended the tradition of spearing grizzlies from boats, leaving bears to do as they pleased.

After the volcanic ash washed away, the villagers returned to hunt and fish at sea but apparently left the swimming bears alone, although Bailey said local residents generally shot any bears they observed. Bears began crossing to coastal islands once again. Bailey found significant reductions in seabird numbers in colonies visited by marauding bears, compared to colonies that had no bear visitors. The predictable and nutritious reward of eggs and chicks made the trip worthwhile. The trait may have sprung up a number of times, starting with short trips to nearby islands, of which there are many. Coastal grizzlies have been seen swimming between rocky headlands and over greater distances to islands. As mentioned, at Brooks Camp, bears crashed into gale-driven waves and retrieved dead salmon from the bottom of Naknek Lake. The density of seabird nests would be especially attractive to a hungry mother with suckling cubs. Bailey estimated approximately 206,000 seabirds from 18 species nesting in the region. Such incentives could establish an annual open-water swim to islands, an innovation transmitted by observational learning and spreading among that population of bears. Annual raids on seabird nests qualified as another cultural pattern, a special calling of the intrepid grizzly.

15

Wild Bears, Wilder Tourists

The fine instincts of that intelligent brute have shown him that it is much easier to get a living from the refuse about the hotels than to forage for it in the wilds of parsimonious nature.

—Hiram Martin Chittenden

How is it that our largest, most magnificent symbol of wildness has been so problematic? Grizzly bears top the list of animals that visitors want to see in national parks. Surely, the vast mountainous landscapes of national parks provided adequate habitat for grizzly bears, whether in the Rocky Mountains or Alaska. Not always, especially in half-tamed Yellowstone National Park, a land networked with roads and developments already spagettified to accommodate millions of visitors in the most productive lower-elevation corridors along streams and piercing up mountain valleys. Meanwhile, declines in bear food, like Whitebark pine nuts and cutthroat trout, no longer draw bears away from campgrounds, roads, and people, where they have the highest mortality rate. In short, food stresses on grizzlies in Yellowstone have set the stage for a new breed of grizzly, one attracted to tons of garbage and food brought by campers to federal lands or around private residences.

Grizzly bears have always been potentially dangerous. Their behavior and intelligence challenges management skills everywhere they occur. Despite an abundance of expert advice, the ability of grizzlies to change their responses to people has remained poorly understood. Informing urban people coming in to grizzly country, especially for short visits, is the most difficult. Some human-grizzly scenarios were only safely manageable if people knew when and how to avoid grizzlies that aggressively defended cubs or a carcass. These encounters were difficult to make harmonious. More broadly, there was a need to re-examine the balance of enjoyment versus conservation, due to the alleged conflict in the Park Service Organic Act mandate. The interpretation has been seriously corrupted by political pressure to advance tourism business interests at the expense of wildlife conservation.

Two problems surface here. The history of national parks revealed the framers' motivation for protection as the foremost priority and aimed to head off entrepreneurs who planned to privatize the land to exploit tourism or minerals. Second, exploding human populations with the affluence and time for travel had overshot the resilience of limited habitats and their wildlife. Millions of people watched zoo-bound grizzlies without negative impacts, but not everyone in America could capture a close-up of a wild grizzly. As the country's population and foreign tourism grew, a comparable growth in park area would have seemed a rational and appropriate response, unless we accept less wild land per person and crowding as the new norm. If this imbalance is left unaddressed, more wildlife will lose habitat, and animals will be displaced from what remains, fractured by more facilities, roads, trails, ATVs, and hikers.

For a century, Yellowstone grizzlies were isolated by an absence of roads, supposedly celebrated but rarely observed. Eventually, nibble by nibble, they were attracted to refuse dumps, complete with bleachers, as park visitation shot up. When the dumps were closed, the grizzlies moved into campgrounds for fresher fare. These bears, raised on stale groceries, lost their wild-feeding ability. When perceived as a threat, upon entering campgrounds, they were shot by rangers. More than 220 died over 3 years in the park and nearby. The behavioral response of dump-raised bears was totally misread by park scientists and superintendents. Independent voices with knowledge and experience with grizzly behavior went unheard. About half the grizzly population was shot. Endangered Species Act protection was invoked to rescue them from oblivion.

To the west, in Yosemite National Park, black bears plagued campers in the bottomlands of Yosemite Valley. As deterrents worked in the valley, the bears followed alpine-bound hikers into backcountry campgrounds, where bears had been historically absent, there to make a living on stolen food.

In 2017, Alaska brown bears returning to Brooks River for salmon were being displaced by twenty thousand bear-loving people. Other bears on Katmai's coast killed two campers in 2003. Plans have proceeded for a massive bridge over tiny Brooks River, while air taxis blanket the beach that bears have used for centuries as their sidewalk to salmon.

Can wildlife survive as rapid encroachment of aircraft, snowmobiles, buses, kayaks, and mountain bikes dominate national parks? A new consideration of the lives of bears, an ethnographic or behavioral approach, has shed light on decades of damage and the effects of management, which has succeeded in getting too many people into parks but failed our wildlife. A wildlife-centered view that employs behavioral science has yet to be tried. It offers a new paradigm for management. This approach challenges the public's and the NPS's ethos that wildlife, even large dangerous carnivores and naïve visitors, can be made compatible. The similarities of all the grizzly and black bear crises touched on above points to a lack of understanding or denial by park managers in putting "visitor experience" and endless growth ahead of wildlife conservation and protection of natural ecological processes. Business interests abetted by political power have encouraged park administrators to attempt the impossible. In Yosemite, naïve urbanites established a camper village called Yosemite Valley while the park attempted to maintain a "natural" population of black bears. History has shown that all visitors will not store their food adequately, and bears, being bears, outwitted people and destroyed property and vacations. The problems continued to arise, and bears continued to die.

Brooks Camp, a commercial lodge with a dining room and bar, a visitor center, and multiple housing units, overlaps a network of bear trails and ancient native artifacts and sacred burial grounds. Every research biologist working at Brooks since 1967 has noted the inappropriate placement of the camp. Perhaps the site was acceptable when small tents and sheds occupied so little space that they were easily avoided by bears and did not disturb the underground artifacts. However, with a much-expanded footprint with over fifty-five buildings strung out along the nearby lake and many more bears crossing the camp, conflicts were predictable and manifestly problematic. Despite millions of dollars spent on an environmental analysis and development concept plans, the best option to move all the buildings across the river was scrapped. Political pressure from financial interests trumped wildlife and archeological protection. Now both sides of Brooks River were slated to have dawn-to-dusk human activity intersecting hungry grizzlies.

Knowing that a Katmai bear dragged two people from their tent and tore them to pieces on the coast, can anyone assure campers that a Brooks bear will not kill and eat anyone in the resort campground? The bears have been surfeited with fish, but how bears will behave if a collapse of salmon occurs is a concern. Alaska's temperatures have been rising faster than elsewhere, meaning that temperatures in streams where salmon spawn will go up. Cold water is essential for all stages of their life cycle. If salmon runs crash, approximately seventy Alaskan brown bears at Brooks will be food stressed and aggressive as they move through camp. Park administrative management has been blocked from putting limits on visitation, creating additional impacts on bears.

No programs have been tested to keep hungry bears from impacting visitors under stressful circumstances. With guns permitted in national parks and ranger accommodations located far from visitor cabins and campgrounds, the possibility of a wounded bear in camp arises. Park policy has been unable to plan for future conflicts that are nearly impossible to solve with current goals.

A recent Katmai "study" purporting to assess current bear management interviewed everyone in camp, including maintenance staff, even the concessionaire's bartender! The report somehow missed interviewing biologists and scientists, who had completed decades of detailed peer-reviewed behavioral studies of the bears and their interactions with people. Those scientific reports and recommendations were sidelined. The most knowledgeable bear research biologist, Tamara Olson, resigned after nine years of onsite experience and study. She met resistance to her rational recommendations from all sides, as did the female biologist before her, Kathy Jope. Kathy had started careful resource management work but left in frustration for greener pastures. I was well aware of her successes in Glacier National Park with grizzly bear research and management. "We have completed a management plan for Brooks for you to look at if you like," Kathy told me early on.

"You bet I'll read it," I replied enthusiastically, partly because of my appreciation that Katmai had articulated their goals and objectives for human-bear interactions in the development concept plan and environmental impact statement. Ultimately, those recommendations were ignored, but Kathy was clear on the factual role that our studies should play.

The value of well-designed studies of bear behavior in national parks can be seen in the insights and success of Rachel Mazur's work described in *Speaking of Bears*. She not only completed an admirable study of how black bears in Yosemite transmit stealing skills to their cubs but also provided an accurate, devastating, yet entertaining, account of the management circus that black bears instigated in the Sierra parks.

Our long-term studies at Brooks employed a systematic sampling of bear behavior to solve problems. Our results were used by Katmai to some extent but openly ridiculed by the lodge owner. At one point, he suggested our research findings "be thrown out the window." Ah, yes, ask the bartender! Better still, follow the money.

So, if readers conclude that more scientific studies seem like a delaying tactic to avoid making politically tough decisions by park administrators, I agree. When park staff made unpopular decisions based on good science, they risked job advancement, especially when well-defined legal mandates governing national parks were pitted against raw political power. That political power lay within the financial self-interest of wealthy corporations and small operators that benefitted from over-exploiting natural areas at the expense of conservation and sensitive approaches to appreciating wildlife. The history of these clashes goes as far back as the inception of national parks. It is beyond the scope of this book to address that discussion, but a thorough and objective account of those conflicts can be read in the book *To Conserve Unimpaired*, by Professor Robert Keiter at the University of Utah.

An encouraging and positive example of the compatibility of bear viewing has developed at another of my former research sites in BC. Our team had superb cooperation from a private ecotourism lodge owner, Dean Wyatt. The experience with Dean was in complete contrast to the anti-science attitude of the Katmai concessionaire, who never approached me or my graduate researchers in all our years of study there. Our work on the BC coast could not have been done without Dean's devotion to bear studies and the high priority he gave to bear protection and conservation. Not only did he host our studies, he also provided accommodation and meals for my students and me over a ten-year period free of charge. Before the beginning of our studies, I wrote a management plan for his operation, which guided their activities. Dean truly wanted to protect the bears. Bear numbers increased each year, a bonus for the owner of a lodge that provided bear viewing. The resort's overnight accommodations were situated on a floating platform, totally away from the estuary and river where bears fed. Bears were left alone in early morning and evening. Guests were guided by certified leaders, and all viewing was done from elevated platforms. When I last visited the site, there were four females in the estuary with four cubs each, a gold standard for superior habitat for grizzlies. Now that is bear watching done right!

16

Teaching Bears Bad Habits and Then Punishing Them

Bears and Honey—Shocking

"Four hundred and Thirty Bears Killed to Save Honey Crop Shocks Province," screamed the *Edmonton Journal* headline in September 1973. The story continued: "Many Albertans were shocked to read that government workers, farmers and beekeepers had joined forces to kill more than 430 black bears in four months in an attempt to reduce damage to honey crops in the Peace River region."

That calamity got me into bears. As a provincial wildlife research biologist, one of my tasks was to research ways to prevent wildlife damage, the politically stormy kind, not the raccoon-in-your-chimney kind. Bears, wolves, and coyotes topped the list of carnivores recognized—sometimes only allegedly—as having economic impacts on agricultural operations. Northern Alberta had premium forested habitat surrounding cropland, making it black bear heaven. Bears left the forest at night to tear into commercial bee yards to get at fat-rich bee larvae.

Farmers and ranchers shot bears on sight, believing that any bear encounter was just days from destroying hives and shutting down their production for the year. Dead bears soon stunk up rural roadsides. My rookie year on the job coincided with an estimated one thousand black bears being killed in Alberta. The public was incensed. Yet so serious was damage from bears that beekeepers monitored their widespread apiaries by aircraft or raced over back roads at breakneck speeds late into the night to intercept them. Without a practical technique, one acceptable by beekeepers, substantial financial losses would continue, and more bears would be killed. A better, non-lethal way to keep bears out of bee yards was needed.

The spread of damage already had the hallmarks of a behavioral epidemic, started by some bold bear innovators, then spreading rapidly through the bear population. Ideally, the solution would be a humane, non-lethal, practical technique to deter bears from entering bee yards and directing them back to natural foods. My previous work in Utah used taste-aversion conditioning. We designed a bear-deterrent study that combined tests of a novel management technique while also helping honey producers fend off bears. This approach is now called experimental management.

My go-getter technician, Larry Roy, and I laid out field-scale trials to compare the effectiveness of two aversive techniques: taste-aversion conditioning versus electric fences. Our large-scale approach had the potential to satisfy beekeepers and politicians. Sixty commercial bee yards were put at our disposal for trials. One season yielded successful results: bears avoided the protected yards. We crossed our fingers that we hadn't just diverted the bears to unprotected farms. Electric fences were more effective than stomach upset from the aversion chemical, lithium chloride.

Bears are brainy enough to learn from a single rewarding experience and file away the food source, a trait that makes them a formidable challenge for state and provincial biologists. With their prodigious strength and curved claws, black bears can escape up large trees, tear dead ones apart, or peel doors off cars. Being widely opportunistic and food obsessed, young bears rely on a two- to three-year food-exploration apprenticeship with their mother, an essential part of their life. They have a big engine to fuel and will consume anything digestible and some that is not. The traditional belief was that black bears eat mainly plants. That was based on analyses of bear scats, but better methods found more animal remains in their diet from both scavenging and predation. As omnivorous carnivores, they eat salmon, rodents (including beavers), deer fawns, and domestic sheep, when the opportunity arises. When natural foods are scarce, bears will investigate any odor, especially human food, garbage, and even bird feeders.

Human-bear conflicts extend back in history wherever bears occur. The Lewis and Clark expedition had grizzlies sniffing around their camps at night along the Missouri and points west. These explorers seemed not to mind that behavior, but confrontations were different. Even though it was risky to shoot a grizzly with a rifle that took almost a minute to reload, bear fat was sought after for frying lean venison, as noted in an earlier chapter. No grizzly injured anyone on the expedition, but many grizzlies were chased and ended up in the pot. Later settlers and others living in bear country had to find ways to avoid depredations, or their supplies got raided. Lethal controls in state after state brought the mighty grizzly to near extinction.

Demanding Bears and Dithering Parks

How is it that the grizzly, our most magnificent symbol of wildness, has been so problematic? Grizzly bears are unmatched among wildlife species that visitors want to see in national parks, especially in Alaska. Haven't the vast mountainous landscapes of national parks provided adequate habitat for grizzly bears, whether in the Rocky Mountains or

Alaska? For more than a century, conflicts with bears have challenged and humiliated national park managers. Making people "bear aware" is challenging, because prevention is a hard sell. When people practiced preventive techniques, progress occurred, but some *Ursus* outwitted the not-so-brilliant *Homo sapiens*. Keeping bears wild, along with the failures and successes of interventions, makes for an interesting story. Parks have been ground zero for large numbers of protected bears coming into contact with inexperienced campers and their marginally protected food.

Like bee-yard bears, the damage that national park bears cause can be serious, especially when opportunities for a food-conditioned bear result in contagious spreading of deviant behavior. You can count on damage to escalate dramatically if newly delinquent bears are ignored, and the problem is not nipped in the bud. If you maintain "it ain't broken," it soon will be. Bears, being the local experts, survive in parks year around. We rank amateurs, as outsiders, have our "superiority" regularly exposed. Sooner or later, a case of public "bearanoia" sets in.

Grizzly bears have been loved or hated, depending on time and place, but they have always had the potential to be dangerous. Their intelligence, ingenuity, and inventiveness have challenged managers' skills everywhere. Despite an abundance of advice from bear experts, how grizzlies changed their responses to people has been poorly understood, especially for informing urban people who come for short visits into grizzly country.

Park service historians, interpreters, and apologists have continued to stress the parks' dual mandate to protect nature while permitting America's 326 million citizens to enjoy their parks. Two problems have bedeviled the enjoyment mandate. Interpretations of the intent of the park framers for establishing public spaces leaves little doubt that protection was a foremost priority to fend off financiers, intent on privatizing the land to exploit tourists or minerals. Second, eased transportation limitations to parks and expanded human populations with the affluence and time for travel overshot the resilience of limited habitats and wildlife. Millions of people can watch a zoo-sheltered grizzly without negative impacts, but not everyone in America, let alone busloads of international travelers, can cop a close-up of a wild grizzly. As noted, as the country's population grew, a comparable growth in park area would have been a logical response, unless we accepted less available wild land per person as the new norm. If this imbalance is left unaddressed, more wildlife will lose habitat and be displaced by more facilities, roads, and trails. Even extreme river rafting, zip-lining, and mountain bike racing have been gaining political traction and priority.

Former wilderness has been half-tamed and trammeled by roads to accommodate millions of visitors. Highways and developments intrude on Yellowstone's most productive land and best bear habitat—those lower-elevation corridors running beside formerly bucolic streams and slicing through mountain-ringed valleys. Meanwhile, crucial foods have declined in remote areas, particularly Whitebark pine nuts and cutthroat trout, staples that formerly drew bears away from campgrounds. Roads and people are death zones for wildlife. Then food stresses on grizzlies in Yellowstone set the stage for a new breed of grizzly, one lured by tons of garbage and provisions brought to public campgrounds and around private residences.

Yosemite National Park was the "World Series" of black bear conflicts in the late 1970s. The park installed storage lockers in Yosemite Valley's large campgrounds, but in the High Sierra backcountry, bears outwitted people and overcame every method used to keep food from bears. Then, into the park rode some Utah State University researchers, intent on solutions.

My enthusiastic graduate student, Bruce Hastings, and I found fertile ground to test aversive techniques for defeating the bandits. But first the bears taught us, the behavior "experts," some lessons. We immediately began losing our food to trained robbers. Bruce started aversive conditioning tests with dilute ammonium hydroxide in stuff sacks, just strong enough and unpleasant enough to douse bears who bit into the packs hanging from tree limbs. Bruce recounted, "It did seem to work in the sense that bears quit using at least one small campground. However, they appeared to shift their efforts to nearby campgrounds. It appeared to work for a location, not the food or food containers." Back to the drawing board.

In the fall of 1977, I stumbled onto a technique to outwit bears while watching lion behavior on television. A young lioness was filmed attempting to crack an ostrich egg with her massive fangs, but they just slid off the hard, curved surface. Eureka! Black bears have similar powerful jaws and teeth. Why not simulate an ostrich egg to store camping food? If containers could resist bear entry, they would get no food, so we figured those bears would quit coming into campsites. We set out to design a cylindrical ostrich egg.

Back in Utah, I cut lengths of plastic irrigation pipe to fit in backpacks, and Bruce returned to Yosemite to test the prototypes. The cylinders resisted all break-in attempts. So successful were these canisters that Yosemite biologists went looking for a manufacturer. It was bear-proof and idiot-proof. Over time, our bear-resistant container proved so effective that parks throughout the USA and Canada adopted them. Some years later, on a visit to Yukon's Kluane National Park in Western Canada, their bear management specialist showed me a shed full of the containers. All hikers were required to carry their food in them. Grizzly bears, he gloated, had stopped approaching hikers when they failed to get food rewards. I did not tell him where the containers came from—or who had failed to patent the design.

Campground Conflicts: Recurring Calamities

In 1997, long after our project ended, Yosemite black bears caused about $2.3 million in damage to visitors' vehicles and other property. Only park employees can appreciate how administrators' priorities changed, but bears didn't. Few people understood the real reason for the onslaught of damage until a park scientist explained the bureaucratic background that had caused the switch. Just before the bear "summer from hell," Yosemite administrators downgraded the importance of bear issues, especially sanitation, staffing, and enforcement of storage rules. Bears responded with a lesson in bear conflicts 2.0. When people let their guard down, bears found all the cracks in the management armor. A new looting culture spread throughout the bear population. Park rangers advised people to store food in their vehicle's trunk. Bears soon solved that puzzle by peeling off locked doors or bashing in windows and burrowing through backseat cushions and springs to get the food. Parking lots were littered with broken glass and debris. In more ways than one, bears ate visitors' lunches while managers ate lunch in their offices.

Bears have large brains and use their intelligence to learn complex adaptations throughout life. Wildly opportunistic, they munch on just about anything that is digestible and some that is not. Folklore and some biologists believed that black bear diets consisted typically of plant materials, but my experience and recent research points more to animal foods. In arid or high-elevation areas, natural foods are seasonally limited, so bears track any interesting odor, especially people's stored food or unsecured garbage.

The stamping into memory of a food type, season, and location seems like imprinting. Cubs observe their mothers closely, share her food, and learn food locations and so develop a tradition. This contributes to individual specialization. Visualize this as a postal route in reverse in which the bears memorize every place to locate food. When they find our food supplies, that same memory kicks in—we start the bear on a life of crime.

Beware! Problem Bear Syndrome Ahead

Decades of bear management in federal, state, and provincial parks confirms that as bears adapt to people to get our provisions, they turn into habitual bag snatchers and become a royal pain in the bureaucracy. The crucial but elusive challenge is to nip a developing problem in the bud. Pity the lowly park biologist when she tried to make her boss aware of a problem that wasn't on anybody's radar—yet. Reactive managers do not fix what isn't broken. But when staff waited for bear damage to reach the threshold of bureaucratic tolerance, action became more expensive, consumed more employee time, and required bear destruction—and possibly cost them their careers. Think of a cascade of waves that ended in a tsunami.

Various ecological factors primed this pump. Bears were constantly hungry, some so severely that they tracked down or trailed anything potentially edible. As opportunistic omnivores with big noses, they traced atoms from organic stuff. Early in Yellowstone's history, food scarcity and handouts lured bears to vehicles and buildings. All over the continent, when berry crops failed, newspapers overflowed with headlines about bear hassles. Bears, naturally, were looking for a substitute food supply.

Animals as large as bears must search constantly for the richest-available food until they accumulate enough fat reserves to survive many months in a den. Recall that the Lewis and Clark expedition killed one big boar that yielded eight gallons of "bear grease." Bear survival in dens has always relied on a hyperphagia, literally "excessive eating." Guided by a specialized taste system, bears are obsessively attracted to oils, fats, and lipids, compounds that are easily digested and metabolically translated into fat that is deposited all over the bear's body. No wonder bears gorge on oily salmon. Earlier in this book, I showed that they can consume over fifteen salmon an hour, which translates into tens of thousands of calories per day. Bears with huge appetites and little natural forage gravitate to garbage or campers' coolers. Unless one loves lawsuits and escalating conflicts, souped-up management is task number one for managers of this creature.

Triggering and Transmitting Learned Traits

Problem bears need only one food reward, and their behavior is rerouted, referred to as "single-trial learning." Once a bear gets hooked on people grub and is then observed by other bears, the trait spreads. Yosemite was the flagship park for these cycles among bears. Despite its pervasiveness, the syndrome was frequently missed until managers faced a crisis.

Most biologists were unaware of how fast foraging tricks swept across a bear clan. An exception was Rachel Mazur's insightful research on social learning among Yosemite's bears. As a park ranger, she tackled spectacular damage to parked cars head-on. A bear "riot" had developed, mostly window smashing and burrowing through backseats, as described earlier. She focused her study on how cubs copied their mothers' behavior—observational learning was the core mechanism of social transmission. Mazur found solid support for this process.

If bears learn rapidly where it is safe to get people food, do they also learn where it is dangerous to seek food? And has that perception been shown to spread among bears? Bears need safe habitat to feed efficiently, especially in traditional locations, like salmon-spawning streams, where they exploit abundant but transient prey. Habitat near roads is alienated and abandoned by bears when risks from armed people are detected. If hunted, are bears made aware that people are dangerous and to be avoided? Arguments on both sides abound.

The suggestion that bears have learned to avoid people because of hunting seems counterintuitive. How can a bear that has been shot learn anything? Sorry, but it's not that simple. Not every bear fired at dies or is even hit by a bullet. Here are some circumstances that account for how bears might learn to fear and avoid people. First, being wounded and surviving. Next, a bear observing a companion getting shot or experiencing its mother being killed or wounded by gunfire. Third, a cub observing and copying its mother's alarm response and running off with her after it witnesses the objects associated with the mother's response. This last type of conditioning is common in many mammals. These mechanisms all contradict the "dead bears can't learn" argument.

How often have animals been wounded and survived? Quite often, it turns out. I have been told that grizzly bear hunters are the worst shots, because their hands shake when aiming (perhaps due to fear or buck fever). It is possible that a high percentage of targeted grizzlies got wounded, escaped, and learned to avoid people. Then there are the cubs or siblings that experienced a companion being shot or wounded. Lastly, if a number of bears were at a food source and one got killed or wounded, observational learning by the others would be another explanation.

Hunting bears has not been effective for minimizing bear conflicts, because problem bears are unlikely to be targeted. However, individual bears can be counter-conditioned if managers have an opportunity to be on site at the time. In 2018, biologists in Yosemite National Park had good luck deterring collared bears, because they intercepted the bears when they approached campgrounds. Incidents of damage dropped precipitously with this staff-intensive approach.

Fitness and Survival Consequences of Food Innovation

Natural selection, as sleuthed by Alfred Russell Wallace and Charles Darwin, resulted in feeding specializations that benefit certain individuals compared to competitors. Abundant food means more cubs, and better cub nutrition means faster maturation, earlier breeding age, and shorter intervals between births and larger litters of cubs. Yosemite backpack food is concentrated, energy-rich, and more abundant than natural foods in the High Sierra's barren alpine zone. One bear we darted, a chronic campground invader, was a super-sized male weighing over five hundred pounds. He was called "Big Ploppy" because of his huge, plastic-laced turds. He exemplified what better food meant for survival. Could a new race of these thieving specialists have outcompeted wild-eating black bears, resulting in a new strain of giant habituated bears? Could we be witnessing evolution in action?

Our Yosemite research centered on bears that immigrated into the High Sierras and became food conditioned to abundant campground fare. Larger bears, like Old Ploppy, got first crack at the concentrated goodies. Large size also favored success in mating competition, another aspect of Darwinian selection, in this case, selecting for big, bad food thieves. Successful monopolization of breeding opportunities worked at the genetic level to promote genes that facilitated ingenious food capture or whatever genetic predisposition engendered these behavioral traits. Less well recognized was the role of a bear's temperament in learning to tolerate close approach to people as a fundamental element of the successful feeding syndrome. So, the combination of new behavioral traits—adapting to people and food conditioning—opened up a new ecological niche, at which the cheeky robber-specialist excelled. The trait spread, became a cultural pattern, and the path of short-term evolution led a portion of the bear population in a new and more successful direction. This process, at a basic behavioral level, underpinned natural selection, because the adaptive behavior had a genetic predisposition component. Over time, through "cultural innovation," these bears were on their way to creating a new subspecies, particularly if they were isolated from others and bred only among themselves. Eventually, the remaining wary, smaller bears would begin to wink out.

Campground bears created major headaches for rangers. Because they could not convince all visitors to secure their goodies, they had to deal with chronic problems. Suddenly, what looked like a trivial problem of a few "nuisance" bears became an outbreak of bears behaving badly. A new type of bear emerged. In time, a phalanx of trained bears overran the park's campgrounds. The new contest pitted trained bears against naïve campers. Home-team advantage went to the bears, who had multiple opportunities to perfect their skills. No surprise that city folk were outwitted. The rangers and even the bear "experts" were no match for the ingenuity of hungry Teddy. Rangers were confronted with a species that could essentially ride a bicycle!

What began as a seemingly minor annoyance transformed through observational learning into a large, expensive, and potentially dangerous problem for managers. Although the problem developed slowly, the end solution was destruction of bears, because they were perceived as a threat to people. Were the bears at fault if they were "trained" by visitors? Inevitably, the agency was responsible and destroyed these animals, which explained the slogan, "a fed bear is a dead bear."

Lessons Learned—Or Not?

Bear encounters are a fact of life in bear country. Long, exasperating experience might have taught people that preventive strategies were needed for the predictable inevitability of problems before managers sank into reactive killing mode again. Wherever bears live near people, better prevention strategies need to be incorporated into all structures, sites, sanitation, and food-storage plans. Local groups had some success with bear awareness programs that promoted securing food and garbage as the first line of defense. Anything less was a nuisance-bear training program. That would be managing human behavior, not bear behavior, the subject of another book.

Yosemite National Park has a long history (or a long nightmare) of trying to educate visitors about black bears. It has turned out to be almost impossible. If you asked Rachel Mazur, or have read her excellent book, *Speaking of Bears: The Bear Crisis and the Tale of Rewilding in Yosemite, Sequoia, and Other National Parks,* it only took about 2 percent of visitors to screw up food storage, and the black bear problems continued. All national parks have a legal mandate to maintain "natural" populations of wildlife, but can anyone expect bears to remain natural when a village of urban Californians sets up tents among them in Yosemite Valley every summer? It required serious tough-on-crime enforcement—one strike, and you're out (of the park). It's not park policy yet, but killing black bears in the Sierra mountain parks *was* policy. Over two hundred bears were destroyed for unacceptable behavior caused by visitors.

Ironically, in all these cases, the number of management kills approached or surpassed hunter kills in jurisdictions that managed hunting in adjacent lands. The same was true for grizzly bears killed in Alberta's Jasper and Banff parks, and the same buried records of the killing, although the numbers of management actions are available. It was the equivalent of having a "sport" hunt in national parks! In the very places charged with preserving true wilderness and bears—the most iconic of species, the animal listed as most desirable to view by visitors—they were not even close to being totally protected.

For Yellowstone grizzlies, from 2002–2007, mortality did not occur within the park but at the periphery. The density of bears declined in the park, and bears migrated outward. Recent analyses by Dr. David Mattson indicate that hunter-related kills were 4.7 percent per annum and livestock-related mortality was an astounding 16.8 percent per annum during the same period, largely on grazing leases on public lands.

PART 4

Science Meets Politics: Wilderness Values, Bears' Future

17

Wilderness Intact

A river is water in its loveliest form; rivers have life and sound and movement and infinity of variation, rivers are veins of the earth through which the life blood returns to the heart.

—Roderick Haig-Brown

A Passion for Place

Brooks River, winding chilly and clear over stones as smooth as eggshells, is liquid heaven. Stream walking is easy on the cobble and pea-gravel bottom, nearly flat for most of its two kilometers from Brooks Lake to Naknek Lake. This cool, curving world is free from silt and volcanic ash, washed in from tributary streams, because Brooks Lake acts like a huge settling basin, spilling only its purest surface waters into Brooks River. The chain of lake-stream-lake sustains a fertile nursery for newly hatched salmon, enriched by the decomposed bodies of their parents' generation and those before. For centuries, this molecular soup has fertilized the upper reaches of the watersheds with ocean nutrients. To some this story may be old hat, but its magic lives on in the salmon cycle. I frame the gift of salmon as vital care packages sent to us from Mother Sea. Alaska has done a better job of salmon management than the federal fisheries agency did way back. They have monitored individual runs of fish, limited obstructive dams, outlawed farmed salmon, and controlled clear-cutting of forests (except in the Tongass National Forest in southeast Alaska, but that is a story for another day).

My first visit to Katmai was in September 1983, fresh from grizzly bear work in Yellowstone and Yosemite. Katmai beamed refreshingly uncomplicated—a pristine river, big bears everywhere, gravelly beaches lined with stunted spruce and alder, all painting an inviting portrait. Its historic log cabins and dirt paths offered a slice of simpler times, when the constructed world didn't mar the landscape. A primitive fishing camp cast a romantic aura, reaching further back into history, when massive bears dominated this wilderness setting. This was real nature, and I found out how real when I struck out on my first hike to Brooks Falls.

Like many field biologists, my science was steeped in the objective facts-only tradition. No room for anthropomorphism to interpret bear behavior. But tracking bears with quirky personalities begged for a looser approach. Were bears really so vicious and despised? Did the perception of bears as furry people need to be so restrictive? Perhaps a more disciplined anthropomorphism, a tentative attitude of empathy, might open doors to the mental lives of these animals.

My wide-ranging observations of Brooks bears during the 1980s revealed novel cultural patterns—their startling behavioral innovations passed on to other bears. Grizzlies deserved to be moved up the ladder with the other big-brained animals that transmitted learned behavior from individual to individual. By 1991 I realized a cluster of bears was targeting one run of salmon, exploiting it doggedly over the Brooks River watershed. As I described earlier, the bears find sea-run salmon at Brooks Falls. At season's end, bears turn back to Brooks to gorge on dying salmon drifting into Naknek Lake. This four-month odyssey of bears tracking tens of thousands of salmon awaited a closer look, before the remarkable bear-salmon story was lost. The onslaught of anglers and monetizing of a bear sideshow degraded Brooks with industrial tourism.

By 1996, when the final development concept plan was completed, national laws, park bureaucracy, and major environmental organizations had not come to the defense of the wonders and mystique of Katmai, a place to inspire those who reject mass tourism. Only courage to confront short-term financial greed could preserve the natural and archeological "resources" of the Brooks River area.

Research—Or More Delay?

In September 2016, Alaskan politicians strong-armed the NPS to renege on its own plans. Ten years in the making, those plans stipulated that the badly sited camp was to be moved across the river, but suddenly, it was allowed to remain in place. Early the next year, a contract was signed for construction of a huge bridge, which included a 1,550-foot elevated boardwalk that served the concessionaire's expansionist interests. Contrary to federal laws and standards for gateway developments, the Secretary of the Interior orchestrated a stealth scenario that encouraged more visitor accommodations and hundreds of air taxi day trips to this tiny gem of prime bear habitat. Maintaining visitor accommodations on traditional bear highways assured continued conflicts with bears and risks to visitors, who walked among seventy or more grizzlies. Some bears kill other bears. Some bears kill people, as happened to Timothy Treadwell and his companion in 2003. The permissive management of bear viewing in Katmai ranks as the least protective of bears compared to all the other six sites in BC and Alaska, where I have worked. Katmai regularly violated best practices standards for bear viewing, as defined in guidelines published by the state and the NPS. There are bound to be knock-on impacts to bears from this commercial power play. The halcyon days at Brooks River are over.

Endangered Spaces

Everything about the Brooks River watershed is big—giant rainbow trout abound, and millions of fingerlings grow into salmon sashimi for eagles, otters, and others up the web. The natural system has worked longer there than the earliest aboriginal migrants, according to discoveries by archeologist Don Dumond, beginning in 1963. For decades, his field team uncovered 4,500 years of human occupation, further testament to the river's richness and productivity. After the end of the last ice age, these first people survived harsh winters in pit-house dwellings and ate dried fish and wildlife from the surrounding seasonal smorgasbord.

Decades after the massive eruption of nearby volcanoes, wartime troops stationed at nearby King Salmon found rest and recreation on the river, a rising star in fly-fishing heaven. Camping quarters at first were crude shacks and tents near the river. They were expanded over a network of bear trails and archeological sites. Lodges and ranger facilities displaced bears' ancient trails from the beach of Naknek Lake on their way to the river. Following an era of world-class fly fishing came ecotourism, featuring big bear viewing close up. To accommodate the influx, cabins sprouted throughout this tiny beach ridge, centered in a wilderness approximately the size of Wales. If parks are for people, this should not have been a problem. Why then, did I not return after so many years and good memories among the salmon bears?

Only a few visitors are aware of how unusual this spectacular concentration of brown bears is around Brooks River. The ham-handed treatment of this unique jewel clobbered my sunny outlook as I processed the physical, ecological, and cultural changes eroding Brooks. Billions of Asians cannot have powdered rhinoceros horn for traditional medicine, and millions of Americans cannot approach wild bears at Brooks River.

Why were bears so locally concentrated and in such numbers? To repeat, Brooks had a unique combination of a super supply of salmon, readily available to a population of un-hunted bears over an unusually long period. Over many decades, these protected bears have learned how to efficiently find and exploit this fish feast, a cultural pattern unreported anywhere else on the planet. Regrettably, future opportunities to investigate these ecological and behavioral mysteries were degraded before the phenomenon was fully understood.

As an ecological treasure, the salmon-bear system concentrated around Brooks River and the lake. The value was enhanced by a fifty-year period of successful restoration of bears that culminated in their current high numbers. Only at these high densities are the bears able to fulfill their role in the ecosystem, highlighted by nutrients pumped into the surrounding forests, berry seeds transported in scats, and other functions yet uncovered. When human activities degrade or eliminate these processes, the park's management goals to protect and preserve natural evolutionary processes are violated. So too is the public interest, because they want the same bounty for present and future generations.

Katmai National Park is one of the world's most important brown bear sanctuaries, and Brooks River is the most important Alaska brown bear concentration in the national park system. It provides critically important feeding habitat for over seventy bears during the sockeye salmon run in July and again in September and October for binging on spawned-out sockeyes.

Each summer, thousands of people come to Brooks River, since no limits exist on the numbers of visitors who arrive by float plane or boat. After arrival and a brief orientation by park rangers on etiquette around bears, visitors are free to walk around the area unguided and unescorted. Most make their way to the security of the elevated platforms overlooking the river.

The NPS has claimed that Katmai is its most important brown bear sanctuary, suggesting that management should be the most restrictive to provide maximum protection of their bears. Conservation might then rank higher than visitor enjoyment. On the contrary, it has the most permissive management of people compared to similar bear-viewing sites. Park planning has been severely derailed, having ignored their own park-funded scientific research for bear habitat protection and bear-human encounters. They have failed to meet federal legal mandates when bullied by Alaska politicians, who have repeatedly interfered on behalf of private commercial interests. The Brooks situation has joined another historical planning fiasco, the Fishing Bridge development in Yellowstone National Park. That site suffered a similar subversion of park planning and public interest in the service of private profit. In 1975, a new development for negative impacts was completed but led to a double-cross when the old site was not removed.

Brooks Camp, as described earlier, began as a collection of small shacks and tents, smack inside a network of active bear trails. Over four decades, managers and researchers recognized that the camp sat too close to bears seeking salmon. Moving it would have alleviated constant and predictable conflicts between bears and people. In 1963, when University of Oregon archeologist Don Dumond began his research, only three bears were seen in July. Obviously, conflicts were far less frequent compared to 2013, when over seventy bears were counted in summer and fall. With cabins, a lodge, a ranger station, and other buildings strung out along Naknek Lake's shoreline, bears passed close to people and structures on their way to Brooks River. Visitors, park staff, and concessionaire employees had close encounters with bears on the shared trails. Brooks Lodge operated a bar late into the night, putting patrons in various stages of sobriety at risk of confronting a bear as they walked to their cabins in the dark.

No Respect

Hatred of grizzlies often runs deep, even among people who had never seen one. We have celebrated a changed belief system about sharks, gorillas, and killer whales, but poor Ol' Griz still carries the stigma of timeworn folklore—that of an inscrutable, unpredictable, treacherous rogue, ever ready to attack and dismember unwitting humans. I experienced personally exactly how fast and powerful they are, rarely granting pardon, if surprised at close range.

Not long after my scrape from death, fortune smiled. A door opened for me to re-enter the bear's world and jump-start my career. In 1983, Katmai National Park casted around for a grizzly ecologist to probe possible peril to their visitors. They were also concerned about human disturbance of the bears at Brooks River. My proposal got the nod, and work with students began. We stepped into a thriving circus of fly fishing and bear viewing in the center of the park. The park's resources manager, Kathy Jope, had some innovative ideas based on her graduate work on grizzlies in Glacier National Park. Kathy backed my proposal. This offer came when I was musing about bear adaptations to people, triggered by recent experiences with black bear mischief in the high country of Yosemite. But a field study, not speculation, was needed to test ideas floating around in the bear community. Few biologists had enough interest in animal behavior to launch a study. Kathy Jope, a rare exception, convinced her administrators to fund a cooperative study. The bonus for me was getting back on the ground again among one of Alaska's densest population of fully protected brown bears, which came to a shallow stream choked with thousands of sockeye salmon.

The growing popularity of Brooks Camp, combined with decisions by Alaska's senators to tolerate no limits on visitor numbers, demanded serious conservation-oriented research for protecting this pristine site. Added to that, 4,500 years of former peoples' artifacts at this exact location had been studied exhaustively by renowned paleo-anthropologist Dr. Don Dumond, rounding out the bear-human saga.

Ancient Wilderness—New Wonderings

Each day I relished the solitude of this small jewel in Alaska's huge wilderness. During lulls in bear and salmon dramatics, I brainstormed about how the ocean's nutrients affected mountain ecosystems and what engines of nature churned away over huge spans of time and space, arcing back to first peoples, first fish, and first bears.

As more bears lumbered in to Brooks Camp, waves of visitors followed. Thanks to Senator Ted Stephens, visitation rose unconstrained over the decade of our research: the chief of pork brought home the bacon. Alaskans, famously hostile to government regulation, welcomed the tourism invasion, which descended on destination resorts, profiting airlines, hotels, lodges, and pilot-guide concessions. Tourism in Alaska increased about 10 percent every year for decades. The conundrum for the NPS was revealed when Superintendent David Morris told me that Senator Stephens threatened to flatline NPS budgets if any federal park in Alaska tried to cap visitor numbers, despite mounting evidence of negative impacts. Katmai became a free for all. Float planes roared in and out from dawn to dusk, crowded the lakeshore, and blocked bears from walking their beach trail along the wilderness lake. A similar rush to see bears was flourishing on the outer Katmai coast, ranger free and easily accessible from Homer on the Kenai Peninsula or from Kodiak, across the Shelikof Straits.

At the same time, a puzzling anomaly played out at nearby McNeil River State Game Sanctuary, a prime bear-viewing site that permitted only ten visitors per session. McNeil's salmon run drew over a hundred bears and many more people than permits were available. If more visitors were permitted, any negative impacts would be undetected, because no studies guided management. Ironically, as the state agency mandated to manage the killing of the state's most popular species in a "sport hunt," it had the state's most restrictive rules about how many people could view bears. Had Alaska's Board of Game shrewdly decided that if bear viewing were limited to a small niche attraction, this activity would have been prevented from expanding and not threatened areas open to bear hunting. That way the state would not have had to deal with a popular attraction: enjoying grizzly bears and photographing them in their natural habitat. Let the feds handle that side of things. McNeil remains a special if restricted destination with common-sense bear management.

Restricting areas for bear viewing functioned in the hunters' interests, opening more of Alaska's wilderness to hunting. Having protection for bears at crucial feeding streams enhanced the number of bears produced. Some McNeil bears moved into hunting management zones and got shot, so places like McNeil River essentially functioned as bear factories. This was deduced from returns of one hundred brown bears immobilized and marked at the falls in 1970 and 1971 by James Faro and others. Their research bears turned up in the fall kill nearby, according to Allan Egbert's 1978 PhD thesis. Later work by Alaska Fish and Game biologists showed clear evidence that the number of bears at McNeil were suppressed every second year due to bear hunting in management zones near the river.

Conversely, our research at Brooks proved bear displacement from feeding sites by people, especially non-habituated or warier adult bears. There was a significant decrease in the activity of this class on the lower river when the lodge stayed open until September 17 compared to 1989, when it closed on September 10, the traditional closing date. This was a natural experiment of human impacts on bear use of the lower river (see note 3). Other habituated bears streamed in, especially families with cubs, honing their skills in capturing big fish. The displaced bears, those least adapted to close contact with people, may have caught fish at night or early in the morning before people appeared. Over time, enormous adult males became more common. The record-shattering density of bears, which concentrated on consistently high numbers of sockeye salmon, posed some intriguing questions. What was the ecological effect of all the fish remains, urine, and feces and the carcasses of creatures decomposing in the forests having on the rest of the ecosystem? Could the extensive migrations of salmon upslope into lakes and streams be replenishing nutrients lost when water eroded them downslope, down to the ocean sink? As noted, we thought of salmon as "care packages" sent by Mother Ocean to her upslope terrestrial children. When visitors saw how excited bears were to catch salmon, they might have felt the same.

In 1991, I imagined these wide-ranging carnivores dropped fish parts and eliminated waste and berry seeds in their timeless tramping along traditional trails. Add a millennial time dimension to the equation, and the enormous scale of the seeding and fertilizing service provided by bears and a hundred other species looms large. This endless nutrient cycling refutes the dogma perpetuated by neo-environmentalist: that people of the Anthropocene have new and superior ways to garden the earth. Are these alternate "facts"? As mentioned earlier, the so-called working landscape of an intact wilderness has always had nutrient pumps in its natural factory that would warm the heart of Henry Ford.

Aboriginal Pacific coastal peoples depended on a landscape salubrious for salmon with its sea-to-land link—not drilled, not dammed, not cleared, not mined, not over-fished—but as the heritage and biological miracle that it had evolved to be. If humans could summon the will to use it rightly and lightly, to fit into cycles like many other mammalian predators, it could be sustained forever. The magic and beauty of this maritime heritage was known but not defended from those ignorant of its workings and benefits.

Scrutiny and Mutiny

Utah's contribution was the last link in a chain of assessments of the impacts of people on bear conservation, which began in 1974. All studies concluded that Brooks Camp needed to be moved to reduce conflicts with bears (see my end notes in this chapter for further reading).

Will Troyer, Katmai's research biologist from 1974 to 1981, described bears causing conflicts cutting through Brooks Camp to feed on salmon. In his 2008 memoir, he referred to his recommendation to reposition Brooks Camp, but the lodge owner opposed the plan and lobbied politicians to block it, according to Troyer. The facilities remained, and so did the owner's obstructionism. By 2017, the conflicts had escalated dramatically. More incidents are summarized in Ringsmuth's 2013 history. All the studies showed displacement of bears and changes in behavior negatively impacting population processes.

My experience and scars earned credibility at Brooks only until our research results ran up against the concessionaire's financial interests. Facts, best practices, and bear research expertise in three parks did not trump raw entrepreneurial political connections. The benefits of moving Brooks Camp across the river were confirmed by every study and aligned with NPS thinking and policies. Regrettably, I discovered that a new-hire biologist had written an internal NPS memo attacking my recommendation to move the camp as being too expensive. He also recommended that my relationship with the NPS be terminated, followed by his takeover of bear behavior research at Brooks. Ultimately, all park administrators agreed to move the camp, until politicians interfered.

A final litany of attacks on our research and borderline character assassination appeared in a 2000 book by retired fishing guide Bo Bennett, who assessed the "university-based" academic's report as unreadable by "mortal humans . . . due to its highly scientific and statistical analysis." Indeed, this former teacher could hardly have read the "misleading" reports while proclaiming "Barrie's personal bias." That bad-mouthing contrasted with the superintendent's acceptance and action on our recommendations. The contrarians dismissed our work and failed to recognize how much scrutiny our reports had been given by independent scientists. The study design and results had survived the students' university committees. The park service had reviewed the results for clarity and relevance. The fishing guide's antagonism toward the park administration was summarized in his chapter, entitled "Are the Inmates Running the Asylum?".

Over time, our project got scores of suggestions from maintenance crews, rangers, concession employees, and even barflies, all anxious to share their opinions on bear management. The wisest source remained resource manager Kathy Jope, author of the park's management plans for bears and people. She had been recruited because of her innovative grizzly research at Glacier National Park. She knew how grizzlies could be managed to adapt to people. Still, a whiff of misogyny drifted from permanent rangers, who had little empathy for bear protection (from my bear-biased position). To them, bear management fell between dominance and a minimum tolerance and at worst complete distain. After thirty years' experience with Katmai, I have little reason to change that opinion, although the crowding and political interference for expansion got more attention and advocacy toward the end.

The backstory on bear-viewing management offers a cautionary tale that contrasts private businesses occupying different land bases in Alaska and BC. The Canadian operation had unrestricted opportunities to exploit bears to maximize bank balances but did not. Management chose to follow a conservation path by limiting access to bears and offering other recreational opportunities for nature-based activities. Almost no government oversight was needed or involved, other than acquiring environmental permits for a floating raft, lodge, and boat fuel on marine waters.

In the Alaskan case, a licensed concessionaire pursued continuous expansion, disparaged official federal planning and environmental assessments, and enlisted powerful politicians with sympathies that favored corporate profits at the expense of conservation. The entrepreneur never funded any studies, rejected facts, and chronically objected to recommendations about bear conservation derived from peer-reviewed government studies. He succeeded in blocking plans that incorporated wide public support after ten years of study and planning. Despite federal laws and regulations mandating protection of wildlife, critical habitat, and evolutionary processes, a private operator overruled the government's conservation planning and increased turnaround visitation. He further expanded the development footprint inside a national park at a time when park policy was to direct future infrastructure and overnight accommodation to gateway communities outside parks.

Now Katmai National Park has extended developments on both sides of Brooks River, and instead of Brooks Camp being relocated, a $9 million bridge, capable of carrying trucks, will link thousands of feet of elevated boardwalk. All funded by government for crowds of foreign and domestic visitors and the financial benefit of a host of businesses licensed to operate on public land. Such is the current face of the 1916 Organic Act's requirement to "regulate the use of the Federal areas known as national parks and leave them unimpaired for the enjoyment of future generations."

18

Science Friction

The fine instincts of that intelligent brute have shown him that it is much easier to get a living from the refuse about the hotels than to forage for it in the wilds of parsimonious nature.

—Hiram Martin Chittenden, *The Yellowstone National Park: Historical and Descriptive*, 1895

Unknown to Overgrown

Landing in Katmai National Park for more research came in the wake of my earlier bear-human interaction studies in Yellowstone and Yosemite. Would more politics surround these brownies? Initially, the inviting camp beside placid Brooks River evoked no hint of conflict among its friendly staff. That was 1984, when the pressure to expand facilities was all but undetectable. Bear management was debated often but amicably. That was before international media boosted bear viewing, bringing boom times, as in lowering the boom on Brooks bears.

Brooks Camp started as a small rustic outpost, adequate for sports fishermen but not for the safety of naïve crowds let loose among a growing population of huge Alaskan bears. By 1986, the need for expansion triggered a development concept plan (DCP). Katmai superintendent Ray Bane stepped up to draft the blueprint. Central to the plan was relocation of the camp from the north side of the river—where escalating ursine encounters had been percolating—to a new location on the south side, away from the bears' busy river corridor. Several cankers festered on the north side, all of which continue to this day.

Visitors and staff collided daily with bears on the network of trails that snaked everywhere. Astonishingly, this had been recognized and studied and reported to the park service for over forty years.

Then there were the precious archeological sites, including ancient graves, that were being disturbed by burying pipes and power lines. The most severe intrusions were from wastewater drainage fields. Also, any trenching and digging for footings resulted in excavations into native artefacts. I observed one of these in 1984, when an excavation for a doorstep yielded a perfectly symmetrical fired-clay bowl, carefully unearthed by park archeologists. A relocated camp would have protected culturally significant and sacred burial grounds from further disturbance.

Lastly, Brooks Camp was being turned into an all-day terminal for air taxis delivering hundreds of day visitors. Dozens of float planes were lined up, wingtip to wingtip, along the shore, which was a busy bear trail. Aircraft were tied to nearby trees by ropes across the beach in an already busy loading and unloading traffic zone, adding to bear-people conflicts. The aircraft, plus ATVs carrying luggage, blocked bears commuting daily from their overnight hideouts to their river dining area. Meanwhile, float planes departed with a deafening cacophony, blasting the entire lower river.

From the start, Ray Bane, a can-do guy, recognized these conflicts and aimed to steer Katmai in a new direction. Our first contact was collegial and memorable. Ray had just tied off his airplane near camp and walked toward me carrying something raw and bloody. Just as he reached me, he threw it at me. It was a gigantic flank steak, fresh from a moose's belly. As park superintendent, one of his duties was to patrol the area by air. He had just circled over Katmai Reserve and spotted some moose hunters about to leave too much meat behind. Ray knew I was a carnivore living on slim rations. Our cookout that night warmed more than the steak. When he said, "Bears come first around here," he stoked a mutual collaboration with me. "You can help me put more science and conservation into park management," was his message.

Laws Matter

Among the park superintendents that I have worked with, Ray Bane stands out. He insisted that the park planning process needed to get the facts straight and up front. The contracted behavioral science studies, under the umbrella of Utah State University, involved graduate research for degrees about bear-human interaction. It had direct relevance for the DCP process at Katmai. Those results also supported the contentious environmental impact statement (EIS). Our behavioral studies thoroughly reinforced earlier recommendations to separate bears from people and overnight accommodations. The park service's line of command included a large planning bureaucracy in Denver, which was at first supportive of Superintendent Bane and facilitated the long, unwieldy process. Ours aligned well with the mandates of the National Park Service's Organic Act. Katmai's bear-management plan also aimed at protecting the activities and habitat of the park's prime attraction, well-behaved brown bears catching and feeding on salmon.

Alaska's senior senator threatened to flatline the Alaska region's budget if any national park in Alaska tried to limit visitation, no matter what the science said about negative impacts on wildlife or esthetic values lost from crowding. Consequently, the service, heedless of its mandate to protect bears, their ecology, their evolution, and their ecosystem, ended up with the most permissive visitor management of any government agency or private bear-viewing operation. Katmai was open season for all. Floatplanes continued crowding the lakeshore, blocked bear movements, and created a management circus in that amazing remote wilderness area on the Alaskan Peninsula. Political pressure had trumped the best science and good planning.

Special Interests and Private Dividends

Soon after the plans for a massive Brooks River bridge received comments from thousands of Americans and others around the world, the plan reached the budgeting phase. Realizing that the NPS meant business, opponents of the plan shifted gears from grumbling and bad-mouthing studies to full-on lobbying of their senators, who, in turn, twisted ears in the Department of the Interior, which oversaw the Service. Some indications of the powder-keg politics involved was described by former US Inspector General Earl Devaney: "Simply stated, short of a crime, anything goes at the highest levels of the Department of the Interior." The apple cart was flipped in favor of commerce and against bear conservation, archeological protection, and the esthetic beauty of serene, silent nature.

Throughout the years of our behavior project, higher bear numbers attracted many more visitors to Brooks Camp. Thanks to the "no limits" edict from Alaska's senior senator, the number of visitors quadrupled over the decade of our research. Tourist bureau counts of visitation to Alaska jumped every year, and that trend continued.

In the official congressional record, Ray read, to his horror, that Senator Lisa Murkowski inveighed against the plan and convinced Interior Secretary Sally Jewell to rescind both the order to move Brooks Camp and to reject the requirement for airplanes to beach on the south side, away from bear traffic. This was contrary to the careful conclusions drawn from biological studies that formed the DCP and EIA, which addressed conservation needs and archeological preservation. It was a gift to the private financial interests of the concessioners and pilot-guides. It put their convenience and financial opportunities ahead of mandated resource protection.

Few people were aware of the chronic antagonism that the Brooks Lodge owner directed at park service managers, the protector of our public lands (on paper). That manager said, "Government feels no loyalty or obligation toward pioneers . . . (they) resent anyone who knows more or has been around longer." That quote comes from a privately published book, *Rods and Wings*, which extols the virtues of those who started fishing lodges on the peninsula. The book's author (mentioned in the previous chapter) had been hired for years by the lodge owner. He attacked the credibility of all the studies that Ray defended and failed to offer any evidence disputing that bears were being chronically displaced. Instead of analyzing our studies in even a superficial way, the author chose to highlight my disfigured face—a reality of no relevance to the real issues.

Ray and earlier park superintendents responded to increasing visitor numbers, guides, and bears by reducing the quota of retained salmon from five to one per day. Ray also required that landed fish be taken in plastic bags directly to the fish house to avoid food conditioning the bears. In the early 1980s, when the limit was five fish, many anglers cached fish on shore within easy reach of bears, a practice that effectively trained bears and alarmed anglers.

Conservation Contrarians

As the interests of most visitors went from fishing to bear viewing, pressure mounted to better manage bear-human conflicts. An early report by park wildlife biologists Tammy Olson and Dr. Ron Squibb was based on over three hundred hours of systematic sampling of bear behavior. Their work, referred to briefly in an earlier chapter, compared bear use in the lower river before and after a one-week extension of the season and lodge closing. The traditional seasonal closing of the lodge on September 10 resulted in a six-fold increase in bear activity among adults compared with a September 17 closing. More significantly, seven non-habituated bears began using the lower river near the bridge when the lodge closed earlier. National park plans to mitigate crowds and noise was being subverted by political interference. Development and private financial interests introduced more noisy aircraft intrusions, which diminished wilderness silence, natural sounds, and degraded the experience for more and more people. So, it came to pass that facts no longer mattered. Detailed planning based on extensive science with broad public input was trumped by opinions from the street. When a bear caught a fish at Brooks Falls, loud clapping and hoots by an entertained public became the norm. Ray's courage and lifelong defense of conservation of the best lands in Alaska earned him the admiration of principled advocates of wild country. It also got him relegated to a desk job at the regional NPS office in Anchorage. He eventually retired, leaving Alaska and the politics that ignored sound conservation principles.

Can national parks be managed to preserve ecological processes if everyone has the right to enjoy sensitive wildlife up close? In Yellowstone, the greatest good for the greatest number collided with reality as busloads of park visitors tried to get close to photograph grizzly bears. When masses of people have the discretionary income to visit remote sites like Brooks River, the impacts multiply. Just as visitors seemed to adapt to crowding and inappropriate human behavior, bears adapted by changing their natural behaviors.

If the amount of public land in wilderness areas were scaled up to match growing population trends, the ratio of land area to citizen might remain the same. However, adding acreage to federally protected land is an uphill battle. In southern Utah and Alaska, efforts to expand public lands were initially met with fierce local opposition. Later, all these unpopular designations proved energizing to local economies. As admirable as the dogged contributions of people like Ray Bane are, it is the plight of visionary ecologists and their depressed followers to mourn the disappearance of a heritage of wild country and its marvellously evolved inhabitants.

PART 5

Imperatives from the Past

19

Sacred Bears: Early Native Ties to Grizzlies

Ancient Eco-Centers: A Tale of Two Carnivores

Just after dawn, I walked alone along the main path through Brooks Camp, listening for bears and anticipating the silvery flashes of salmon in the river ahead. This pristine scene harkened back to humankind's first contact with bears before there was a constructed world. Magical. Clues of the primitive past were revealed in scattered earthen depressions of ancient houses. Dozens of pit houses or barabaras, so dense that any random dig jars the ghosts of earlier people, harvesting and drying fish for a long, dark winter. Bears too came for the salmon harvest, storing them under their skin to survive the cold winter in another dark house.

Brooks Camp is the site of the largest and best-investigated archeological site in Alaska. During two decades of excavation, starting in 1960 along Brooks River, retired archeologist Dr. Don Dumond made exciting discoveries about early Yup'ik people. Dumond led a team from the University of Oregon, discovered a village of pit houses occupied for millennia until the arrival of Europeans. From a few settlement sites and locations where salmon were caught on the Peninsula Dumond made inspired predictions about narrow landforms at stream entrances that would yield Yup'ik villages and artifacts. Brown bear aggregations at these same sites probably guided the first Alaskans to ample fish in summer and where to build winter houses. Brooks River presented an intact, rare, and dramatic example of the ancient past, replete with fish and tolerant bears—bears undeterred by guns of fearful Europeans. Among the rich collection of tools and bones from mammals, fish, and humans, the archeologists reported almost no grizzly bones, suggesting that hunting and eating bears was rare or absent. This fits with the hypothesis of native co-existence with bears, but it little more than speculation. Similarly, in recent times, the park's protected bears quickly learned that people were no threat and adapted to fishing among guides and rangers.

The coexistence of bears and Aleuts, Athabascans, and Yup'ik people on the Alaskan Peninsula lasted at least the 4,200 years that people occupied fishing communities at the Brooks River site. No doubt, bears and people caught salmon in the same locations. How could this have happened? An explanation of co-existence was needed. The interactions that we have now with the bears may provide clues to the relationship of that period.

Grizzlies and Plains Indians at Buffalo Jumps

North American Plains Indians harvested bison by driving them over cliffs for thousands of years. In southern Alberta, I visited Head-Smashed-In Buffalo Jump, one of the best reconstructions of how this cultural pattern worked for over six thousand years. The effort required to build stone cairns, enclosing guide lanes five-kilometers long to channel stampeding bison, was truly impressive. Equally impressive were the tactics these people used to ensure that all the animals went over and none turned back.

On first reflection, this may seem like a flawed conservation strategy. Why overkill your culture's essential supply-store species? First, I considered that any tribe that invested so much effort—decades of moving stones to build a line of cairns—had to make certain that the animals did not learn about the trap, balk at the opening, and turn back. That would happen if some bison were driven toward the cliff, remembered escaping an earlier trapping attempt, and turned back. This kind of harvest only works if the drive kills all the animals. If there are survivors, they communicate warning signals when joining other herds. They would have sensed the trap and led others to balk during the next season's drive. This is not idle speculation. In East Africa, a similar behavioral reaction was experienced when game ranchers tried to drive and trap wildebeest in corrals in successive years. Once bitten, twice shy. One game-ranching company realized their traps were rendered ineffective if they had any escapees from the drive.

After natives drove bison over a cliff, they butchered dozens of dead and dying bison piled at the base of the cliff. Despite the need to process the meat without delay, it was too much work to finish in a day or two. During the day, the carcasses were stripped of meat and taken to be dried over smoky fires at their encampment, probably some distance out on the prairie, well away from the cliff.

Would the Great Plains grizzly, a big, aggressive carnivore, have come sniffing around buffalo jumps looking for a share of this mountain of animal flesh? At the bottom of the cliff, armed hunters and their dogs were ready to defend the spoils if bears or wolves approached during daylight hours. After the hunters left for camp, the grizzlies could feed on the remains, secure from conflict and harassment from dogs and people, although still competing with wolves. Grizzlies always contended for a share, even if the prey was killed by wolves or another smaller bear, but they preferred to feed without risking injury.

That is a likely scenario, based on what historian Paul Schullery ferreted out from the Lewis and Clark journals. He quoted expedition member Whitehouse's observations that wolves and bears "feasted on the remains" after the natives took what meat they wanted. This confirms that bears and people shared the large communal kills. This situation is similar to Paleo-Indians at Brooks River drying salmon. Bears and people likely feasted together on huge salmon runs.

Anthropologist Dr. Jack Brink, author of the comprehensive and definitive book, *Imagining Head-Smashed-In,* is a foremost scholar of this site. In personal correspondence, he generously responded to my question of grizzlies near people there.

> To my knowledge, we have no scientific confirmation this happened. I have no doubt grizzly bears came around the kills shortly after the event. There may have been occasional contact and conflict, though we know people deeply feared the bears and would have been extremely careful. I picture many large cooking fires blazing night and day in the camp. In my book.... I have noted a number of entries about Plains Grizzly.

Surprisingly, we saw similar behavior among adult male bears at Glendale River, BC, coming to a stream weir for salmon only after the day-visitors had left. These bears gave every indication of a distinct aversion to people, possibly from being hunted or injured while escaping poachers' traps.

At bison jumps, bears and people no doubt learned to avoid each other but still shared piles of meat, innards, and bones. Over time, stalemate became the norm as both cultures tried to avoid conflict. In many ways, this has parallels with Kung bushmen contending with lions to share carcasses, as told by author Elizabeth Marshal Thomas. The lions realized that gangs of people with spears could injure them, so they waited their turn. Bears are capable of the same adjustment. To avoid conflict, subordinate bears that came to Brooks Falls waited for a dominant bear to catch a fish and take it into the forest to eat. Both succeeded by patiently adjusting. Did these primal people benefit from observing grizzlies? Our growing appreciation of grizzlies' impressive brains and their cultural adaptations to finding enough food to support their size presents a pattern that early people likely mimicked.

Where Modern Native Bands Live Each Day with Bears

Rain poured down all morning in Wannock River, a village of the Oweekeno Nation in Rivers Inlet on BC's central coast. Offshore of the town wharf, we had anchored our small trimaran, home base for surveys by a group of bear conservationists from Round River Conservation Studies. We motored our rigid-hulled inflatable boat against the tide and rushing outflow of the Wannock River to land at the village dock.

Lacking an invitation into the village, we introduced ourselves to a hospitable Oweekeno fisherman and stood on the dock talking for an hour in a downpour. The conversation drifted to how villagers responded to bears in town, not a rare event, because their village had sat for hundreds of years right on a major bear trail. The village was located strategically at the outflow of a major river drainage but was hemmed in by high cliffs right behind it. With no alternative passage for man or beast, encounters were predictable and had been for hundreds of years.

These contacts occurred wherever humans intruded on salmon streams. On Brooks River, I watched the surfacing fins of schooling salmon and anticipated the animals that would soon exploit this wealth. Nature abhors a vacuum; bears would be there to suck up salmon. Initially, I concentrated on the behavior of individual bears, but as I saw bears accommodating so well to people everywhere, I began to visualize bear cultures analogous to native cultures. Mothers brought their cubs to the rivers, and those cubs would likewise bring their cubs—a learned, transmitted pattern became a cultural tradition. How was conflict with the aboriginal people resolved? Wherever grizzlies existed near people and wild food, the bears had a way of getting some, even at some risk to their lives. Salmon were captured by people and bears at similar sites—waterfalls, riffles, and outflows into lakes. Whereas bears eat their catch immediately, historically, people dried most of their fish for winter storage by hanging fish on racks in the sun or smoking them. This had a disadvantage that the fish were not secured from bear robbery. Studying current bear behavior suggests ways ancient people defended their caches.

Following the Grizzly to Food

Where suitable habitat remains in North America, grizzlies still roam widely. The high, wild country offers a challenge to those who seek to follow and observe them. Grizzlies range over rocky, icy, brushy, swampy places at ankle-breaking speed for humans. They do not welcome accompaniment. An exception was the intrepid outdoorsman, Doug Peacock. In 1975 he set off to film grizzlies high in the Apgar Mountains of southwestern Glacier National Park. Despite more than a few charges, he came to recognize many grizzlies and how to approach them.

Two years later, in early summer of 1977, I hiked that same area with a pistol-packing park biologist, Cliff Martinka, who pointed out hillsides blanketed with lush huckleberry patches flourishing after wildfires. When we approached a fresh den, Cliff confessed that he would not hike on these park trails with his family. Since I was looking for a reliable site to observe grizzlies near hiking trails, Glacier National Park did not appear very promising. Very good bear habitat, but following bears would be tough and maybe dangerous. I decided to keep looking.

Good locations for prolonged observation are where bears aggregate in shallow salmon streams. In 1984, I lucked out with a small group of easily identified bears at Brooks River on the Alaskan Peninsula. These bears tracked schools of salmon through every stage in their spawning cycle across watersheds. Their efficient tracking furnished the perfect food all summer and fall, one of the longest periods of access among salmon-blessed Alaskan bears. Early people and bears must have inherited this hunter-scavenger culture, because the Brooks area soon supported an exceedingly dense population of grizzlies, unmatched anywhere on Earth. Such is the payoff of learning and remembering where the kitchens are.

Although bears have excellent noses for unearthing hidden or buried food, it takes learning and memory to know consistently where to go. No other places have as rich and concentrated food as salmon streams. To repeat earlier observations, the Brooks region is unique for the length of time that one run of fish is accessible to bears. Many Pacific rivers have salmon but not the falls or shallow water to make fish accessible. In mountainous Yellowstone Lake, introduced lake trout are not vulnerable to grizzlies, because they live and spawn deep in the lake, unlike the disappearing cutthroat, a native stream-spawning trout.

What challenges do other grizzly populations face to locate food, especially with climate change? Can they keep track of changing feeding sites in the Rockies when there is such unpredictability in factors like dispersion, nutritional value, and accessibility? An example of the survival skills needed by a grizzly, also a challenge to first peoples, includes judging the quality, quantity, and accessibility of food. The quantity of a food item tops the choice list. Small patches of a few berries aren't worth exploiting. If abundant but not easily accessed, bears don't bother. Berry bushes that are productive but dispersed widely in small patches are not worth it either.

Predictability and renewal rate of seasonal foods is critical. Whitebark pine nut production, for example, is extremely variable from year to year. In a poor year, do bears remember other fall foods that have the protein, fats, and oils found in pine nuts? The rate of renewal of a food is another important characteristic that is maximized in schools of salmon. For every missed fish passing through, another charges upstream. Instead of fighting for a fish or defending turf under these conditions, bears can just wait or search elsewhere. Berries, on the other hand, have a renewal rate of zero. If a bear mistimes its arrival, birds will finish the berries off. A bear's ability to remember when and where edibles are stocked pays off. Another feature that can be overlooked is whether items are durable or if they decay quickly. Last are ephemeral prey that require exquisite timing for capture—newborn elk, for example. They are vulnerable for only the few days when they lie alone until they are able to outrun bears. Newborns rank as a fugitive food requiring recall of birthing time and locations. Similarly, good timing is required for feeding on spawning cutthroat trout when they occur widely in any of Yellowstone Lake's fifty-two spawning streams. This was a significant feeding niche for many grizzlies until cutthroat trout populations were decimated by lake trout, an introduced predator.

Another dimension of habitat, frequently misunderstood, is the security of habitat from the rapid proliferation of trails, roads, and off-road vehicles that provide access to armed people, a new threat to bear existence. Historically, security or effectiveness of habitat could be taken for granted in assessing habitat quality, because fewer people entered wild country. If a wary bear senses danger, it forgoes feeding in that habitat. This subtle psychological feature of habitat is applicable to all types of food gathering. Biologists mapping bear habitat can no longer rely just on forest cover but must develop a map layer of relative security. If a bear disregards security or does not sense risks, the habitat can become an attractive trap and eventually a mortality sink. This was the tragic scenario after early American contact with our great bear and, unlike the coyote, was not resolved by bear adaptation or a stalemate.

You might think that, after fifty years of research on this iconic carnivore, our work is done. On the contrary, the question of the efficiency of bears to exploit their habitat and their success in stoking that furry furnace for six months in a den still offers challenges. The ancients observed and copied the great bear, surely one reason to value and respect him. Whether a guide for indigenous people to find reliable edibles on a new continent, the feeding behavior of native animals was just the template needed to forage effectively. Small wonder that bears served as all-knowing tutors and elicited reverence for their ability to get fat and survive so well. Sacred indeed.

Tolerant behavior in bears goes hand in hand with superabundant salmon and little competition. Would food-stressed Rocky Mountain grizzlies have been less adaptable and more aggressive to people historically? As emphasized in chapter three, a careful reading of Lewis and Clark's journals reveals some astonishing insights. These are the earliest sources of precise descriptions of grizzlies' responses to every imaginable approach by humans, a rare gift.

Few reviewers of the journals recognized that grizzly bears were a source of cooking fat and calories, not an ominous threat. But settlers with sheep and cattle greeted bears with traps and poison, leaving so few that hardly any pioneers or their descendants had direct experience with them outside of national parks. The population in Yellowstone has rebounded somewhat from its appalling government decimation in the 1970s. Recovery is tentative, because threats to their food and security still exist, especially in the road-blitzed public lands around the park, now teeming with armed Wild Westerners. When the park dumps closed, about half the grizzlies were killed. Trapping, collaring, and monitoring continued for the next forty years. From an animal behaviorist's perspective, this constitutes sanctioned harassment of park grizzlies in the name of management of an endangered species. From a bear's perspective, this amounts to about one hundred years of adapting to aversive treatment by people. How much of an aggressive disposition in bears was stimulated is hard to say. No one asked the question, but we can speculate. If their behavior is compared with that of protected Alaskan bears, there can be no doubt that Yellowstone grizzlies have developed an attitude. It is not too late to address the effects of mismanagement on these grizzlies, especially with the continuing pressure on the federal government to remove Yellowstone grizzlies from the list of species protected by the Endangered Species Act.

Yellowstone bear managers have closed areas to visitors as a precaution since 1986. Kerry Gunther, the current bear specialist, explained that this was done "to prevent displacement of bears from prime habitat during a critical period." For example, Pelican Valley was closed in the mid-1980s, when there were still abundant trout in streams around Yellowstone Lake in which grizzlies could feed. About that time, I served on a "blue ribbon" committee that recommended restrictions on visitors, so bears could forage undisturbed. Why these bears are so sensitive to human contact, totally unlike Katmai grizzlies, is a phenomenon that awaits examination.

Gunther, in his thesis on Pelican Valley activity, recorded 961 sightings of 1,382 bears over five years. From the top of Pelican Cone, behavior of bears about 1.6 to 12.1 kilometers away was tallied. Of nineteen confrontations with people, eighteen were of bears being displaced over sixty-eight meters. Of the five charges witnessed, all were by females with cubs from that year. In general, bears stayed near cover and avoided occupied campsites. This is evidence that Yellowstone's grizzlies were relatively intolerant of humans. Gunther did mention four bears that appeared to be habituated to people on trails, an indication that behavior adaptation to people was beginning. Current management is far more tolerant of habituated bears, a good thing, as they can now benefit by having access to habitat near trails and roads.

It may be significant that none of bears that Gunther observed were collared bears, so they had no capture effects on their behavior. Pelican Valley was passed up for bear trapping, so nothing is known about prior contacts with people, negative or positive. However, bears in this population could have had a delayed intolerance response to people, similar to the Addo elephant culture that came from attempts at culling, as described earlier. This hypothesis needs testing, especially considering the decision to remove ESA protection. Keep in mind that whenever bears leave the park, whether to avoid crowds or seek food, such as livestock or elk hunter offal, they are exposed to illegal hunting, not to mention some questionable "defense of life" kills by frightened armed people. This will significantly contribute to create wary bears, leading to a culture of cryptic behavior. In an increasingly crowded Yellowstone ecosystem, people shyness has concomitant costs for bears in terms of survival, reproductive rates, and long-term conservation.

20

Bear Viewing Takes Flight

Tunnel Vision Tints Views on Viewing

If you wanted to watch bears in the early 1980s in North America, there was only one site— Alaska's McNeil River. It was *the* place, especially for photographers. Utah State University behavior studies began there in 1970. As a recreational attraction, bear viewing had a low profile, even among biologists with broad experience of black bears and grizzlies. Few were familiar with how protected bears, with a surfeit of salmon, adapt to people and our food caches. The food-conditioning syndrome received much more attention. When hungry bears were attracted to people's coolers by odors and were rewarded, a chronic problem grew increasingly worse in Yellowstone and Yosemite national parks.

Bears are ravenously hungry when salmon are unavailable. Grizzlies in Denali National Park, for example, were observed feeding for eighteen hours a day in summer and fall, an indication of their hunger in preparation for winter denning. However, Brooks bears had a surfeit of their preferred food, premium salmon, so our groceries and garbage were far less attractive. This very different relationship was not recognized by government bear biologists, who had generalized that habituation always leads to food conditioning, which leads, they said, to such bears being killed as threats or nuisances. The erroneous belief that higher mortality always follows habituation became an impediment for permits for bear viewing in BC. Entrepreneurs saw an uptick in demand and wanted to add bear viewing as a non-consumptive way to appreciate, understand, and protect declining grizzly populations. Resistance to viewing was also seen as a threat to bear hunting. Willful blindness about salmon-bear behavior dominated discussions of management alternatives. I experienced a dose of that when our published results were misinterpreted, maligned, or cherry-picked by government biologists, commercial park concessionaires, and BC hunting organizations.

Starting in the late 1990s, wildlife branches in BC and Alaska were the center of controversies over the effects of bear viewing with the expansion of private and government watchable wildlife programs. Clashes arose between bear-hunting interests and resistance to increasing non-consumptive recreation. Opposition in agencies based on tradition and the entrenched personal belief systems of government biologists caused much-publicized conflicts. Then bear management became intensely political. With the cessation of trophy hunting in BC in 2017, discussion of the controversy over bear viewing may now seem moot, but it has remained germane. This is because the clash of values continues between the majority of the bear-appreciating public and the beliefs of grizzly hunters, guide-outfitters, lobbyists, and the BC biologists who sympathize with and serve hunter interests.

In the BC government's 1995 report on grizzly bear conservation, the position on bear viewing was that the "mere presence of humans in grizzly bear habitat can have an impact on bears," It alleged that viewing "may cause a bear to lose its natural fear and avoidance of humans".

Leaving aside for the moment the unexamined assumption that wild, un-hunted grizzlies always fear and avoid people, the position that watching bears causes unacceptable impacts while snaring, drugging, and collaring them for research is acceptable defies logic and experience.

The government's assertion that as bears become habituated to people, they routinely approach people seeking food or damaging property is incorrect. That linkage only occurs in specific situations. In short, the idea that habituated bears always become food conditioned, causing their destruction as "problem animals," was an untested hypothesis that grew into a flawed generality. That this was the government biologists' contention is indicated by this excerpt regarding bear viewing: "Although the absolute impacts of displacement and habituation are difficult to quantify, it is *certain* (emphasis added) that highly habituated bears have a higher probability of mortality."

Missing in this interpretation is recognition that well-fed bears at salmon streams do not search for anthropogenic food when habituated to people (although carelessness with unsecured food can certainly hook a salmon-eating bear). They have more than enough salmon to eat, so they just adapt to people. That's why there is no unusual threat or significant damage from these bears and no increased mortality results. In fact, the opposite is true.

If this is the case on salmon streams, why do some academic and government biologists continue to maintain that viewing leads to mortality in bears? Unfortunately, neither of the biologists that had contrarian views carried out or supervised any empirical studies of bear viewing. Furthermore, none had ever visited any bear-viewing sites, examined the certified best-practices programs, or referenced peer-reviewed papers reporting long-term behavioral investigations of the Katmai bears. Biased conclusions were developed from places and situations quite different from well-protected sites, like those in Katmai, McNeil, and coastal BC rivers, where bears were well fed.

Returning briefly to the BC government's report covering bear viewing on the northwestern coast, I objected to their conclusion that bear viewing was hugely negative, because the report confused situations in or near mountain parks, where bears die mainly from human causes, such as management policies, vehicle accidents, mistaken identity, and depredation conflicts, compared to very different situations on the salmon streams of BC and Alaska. I also pointed out misinterpretations of our published research (three studies in BC over six years and four studies in Katmai National Park over nine years). The community advisory committee's lead government biologist seemed to be under considerable pressure to cherry-pick information that gave a negative assessment of bear viewing, because it posed a threat to bear hunting. This notion gains support from recent sociological studies that pointed out a mindset among conservation officers and policy makers that favored hunting despite a mandate to protect bears as a public trust for all the public.

This controversy might seem to stem from a simple oversight or lack of experience with bear-viewing operations. However, while some of our research was cited (incorrectly) as the major information source, I was not invited to review reports. Finally, rather than correcting their report, the entire discussion section on bear viewing was deleted. The facts did not support their preordained policy.

By 2017, over sixty nature tour businesses in BC offered bear viewing. With economic multipliers factored in, opportunities to watch bears were twelve times more valuable than bear hunting. Shoot a bear, and only one person takes a skin home. Protect that bear, and a thousand people can enjoy it alive, learn something, and have an experience and photographs to last a lifetime.

Another argument offered against viewing was the government's allegation that bears would be disturbed, but the same argument was not made for hunting. Furthermore, why was the effect of poaching, resulting from inadequate enforcement, not a concern to government biologists? While on the Glendale River bear-viewing platform, we observed three crippled grizzly bears over a two-day period, one having lost a hind foot. This was reported to have resulted from illegal trapping in an adjacent inlet. Then followed a complete disappearance of all large male bears at the salmon weir below the viewing platform. Such serious habitat alienation for these bears is a severe impact that needs enforcement attention.

When our Katmai work began, no hunting issues were looming. Only the calm end of the spectrum was highlighted—bears totally protected from hunting and capture, the same protection for habitat and allied interest in maintaining evolutionary processes, all primary goals of NPS management.

My first visit to Katmai National Park was by floatplane, piloted by the park superintendent in the fall of 1983. Lifting off King Salmon River, we flew for an hour over endless ponds and muskeg until Brooks Camp loomed ahead, bordering a sparkling lake and a sandy beach. Visiting in fall, a quiet time, sure beat summer in camp, burgeoning with visitors from all over the world plus park staff and lodge employees. Rangers had instituted a new bear-management plan, which was more like a people-management plan, to meet current needs. Seasonal human-bear encounters along the river were mostly harmonious, except for a few adrenaline-charged contacts. The bears had long ago accommodated to wading anglers and meandering visitors. Their attacks were aimed at salmon.

The park's management plan passed muster until visitor numbers lurched skyward, which raised concerns about threats to bears' use of the river and getting too close to people, especially foreign tourists, who were especially unprepared to interact with Alaskan grizzlies. The new ten-year plan needed reliable information about Brooks bears' responses to the coming onslaught of visitors. This meant documenting bear-human interactions of all kinds. Thirty-four years of research on bear-human interaction in Alaska and BC anchor my personal insights to counter misguided opinions and generalities about the effects of viewing bears.

A first surprise at Brooks Camp was the stunning compatibility of so many bears with the constant traffic from employees, photographers, and observers. This contrasted radically with my former experiences with mountain grizzlies in Yellowstone, Glacier, and Banff as well as black bears in Yosemite, where bear habituation to people had led to easy food conditioning, unless food was stored securely by all visitors, a condition rarely achieved.

How Bear Viewing Is Best Done

The response of wild bears to humans at wildlife-viewing venues can be negative, neutral, or positive for the bears, depending on several conditions. Prior experience of bears with people ranks near the top and, if negative, resists adjustment. Learning to adapt to people plays a central role in every location. When bears have a history of negative experiences with humans, the initial impacts are magnified, which sounds like common sense. In the case of coastal Pacific bears that have not been hunted for many decades, (e.g., McNeil Falls and Brooks River), habituation occurred rapidly to the benign presence of people—faster if the visitors were guided and supervised by someone who could read bear communication.

In contrast, bears that have been subjected to hunting, snaring, or harassment respond with exceptional sensitivity to the presence of people by withdrawal. If the presence of people has been repeatedly disturbing, then displacement from that specific habitat results. This is known as habitat alienation. Bears generalize negative experiences with hunters to other people, who have no intent to harm them. However, drawing broad generalizations from these situations is risky.

To be considerate of bears at Glendale, viewing was limited to five or six midday hours, leaving most of the twenty-four hours for undisturbed feeding. Visitors at Pack Creek, McNeil River, and Glendale River were led by experienced guides. Visitors at Brooks River were far more intrusive, because many stayed overnight in cabins or a campground and could encounter bears from dawn to dusk. Returning to their cabins at night from the lodge or bar could easily result in a meeting on the trail.

Bear viewing tours in BC have provided various procedures to lessen disturbances. Walking on shore had no support, so when bears were feeding on sedge in estuaries, the lodge brought in viewers by boat. When bears were present at the upstream weir in Glendale River, observation took place from an elevated platform. Ground-level observation and photography were never permitted, because bears approached from all directions to fish for salmon.

Impacts on bears were predictable and mitigated when viewing operations were based on simple monitoring that was focused on management issues to guide policies and training. Katmai National Park has an admirable record of supporting independent research to guide bear viewing. But for a private operator, Knight Inlet Lodge was unique as a Canadian business, funding years of independent research directed toward conservation management. At Brooks, unfortunately, a chronic conflict was evident, laid out in Katherine Ringsmuth's history of bear management. Concessionaires benefit from the National Park Service's maintenance, guiding, and operating costs of facilities, but the businesses reap windfall profits.

Stewardship and appreciation of coastal brown bears is not advanced when biologists promulgate misinformation and negative attitudes about the effects of viewing. It is clear from a raft of research and long experience with successful viewing programs that growth and productivity of bear populations is promoted. Viewed populations of bears are well managed, and visitors are guided by experienced people, partly because it is good for business. Due to the increased presence of people, bear viewing also reduces illegal killing, especially in areas that have little state or provincial monitoring or enforcement at sites.

Bear-viewing sites have been perceived to be in conflict with bear hunting because of the incompatibility of the two activities at the same location. More serious are the ethical concerns about shooting bears that have learned to trust people. Such critics of bear viewing would do well to review programs at Kodiak National Wildlife Refuge in Alaska. They might then understand how such activities can be compatible by designating separate seasons for each and then establishing protected zones around viewing areas. Likewise, at McNeil Falls, bears have been protected from hunting since 1967, although some of the regular bears have been shot legally when they ventured off the refuge into surrounding hunting zones. These bear kills were known from numbered ear tags, as well from the kill rate being unusually high in the game-management units around the refuge. Biologically sound methods for compatibility are available if management objectives aim to meet the recreational interests of a variety of users rather than continuing to serve only the narrower interests and small clientele of grizzly bear hunters. With the cessation of grizzly bear hunting in BC, bear viewing is no longer a threat to the hegemony of the guide-outfitters or grizzly bear hunters, unless class-action lawsuits influence wavering politicians. In Alaska, the rationale for protecting grizzlies at streams was recognized as important by biologists in a source-sink framework that recognized the value of salmon stream contributions to healthy populations. Managing carnivores can be very productive for the population by protecting the source-breeding segments of bear populations that constitute the core of bear reproduction.

Good Food Means Good Bear Behavior and Safe Bear Viewing

Bears exhibit amazingly wide variation in their behavior toward people depending on their habitat (meaning the food base and its security), their experience with humans (free roaming or trapped), and the degree of protection they have received throughout their lives. Whether viewing of bears in wild country causes displacement or disturbance depends on the kind of historic relationship humans have had with bears. Here are some settings and conditions where impacts are minimal or positive for bears.

Common sense might have convinced us that impacts of human approach are least in places where bears have been protected for decades, and enforcement of illegal killing is effective. Brooks River has strived for such considerate management of viewing without intrusive handling of bears (except one short capture project in the 1960s). Katmai's bear monitoring through the 1980s and 1990s documented a rapidly growing population of bears attempting to adapt to throngs of anglers, fishing guides, and photographers during the summer and fall. No indications of food limitation occurred (e.g., no skinny bears and no decline in cub production). With some notable exceptions, increasing numbers of people were tolerated as the bear population increased. However, focused research and subsequent monitoring by park biologists demonstrated that a significant segment of the bear population was less tolerant of people and did not appear on the river during daylight hours. Also, the Septembers when Brooks lodge was closed a week later than the traditional date resulted in fewer bears recorded during that extra week, compared to the shorter period the year before. Each year the number of bears shot up as soon as the commotion of the lodge closure, floating bridge removal, and employee departures wound down.

Among biologists only familiar with more food-limited populations of grizzlies in mountain parks, such as in Banff, Jasper, Yellowstone, and Glacier National Parks, a different perception locked in. There the effects of habituation on grizzlies had serious consequences on occasion. Unwary bears began to associate food with people and ventured into campsites. Lacking fear of humans, they were predisposed to come into camps and take food where they could find it. It is crucial in managing grizzlies to understand that bears can become very aggressive in their pursuit of food, although they rarely prey on people. Habituation by Yellowstone's roadside bears is an exception to this effect, in that they become habituated to vehicles and people jumping out of cars with cameras. So far this lack of wariness has not developed into problem bears entering campgrounds, because there has been no artificial feeding. Still, there is a major problem with people when they jump out of cars with cameras blazing. Bear jams occur, traffic is snarled, and visitors stray far from their cars.

The problem scenario linking habituation and food conditioning has rarely been observed in Alaskan salmon bears at sites like Brooks Camp, even though campers and bears share the same areas. It seems obvious that people-habituated, salmon-eating bears do not approach people for food because of the ample food in the rivers. In the fall, with people absent, bears have broken into buildings when attracted to odors, so buildings are now protected with electric fences after fall shutdown. These bears have not approached people aggressively for human vittles, but some will certainly follow people with a fish on the line. This behavior is discouraged by requiring anglers to break their line or take a landed fish immediately to a fish house. For bears that are persistent in tracking anglers, rubber bullet punishment has proven effective. Unlike mountain bears, Brooks bears do not approach and intimidate people to get snacks. Thankfully, the situation of bears being killed for aggressive food seeking is not a source of mortality for bears in national parks like Katmai, but it does happen in mountain national parks. Hence the conclusions reached by Dr. David Mattson and colleagues that the unwary or somewhat habituated bears in the Yellowstone ecosystem have a higher probability of approaching people, resulting in their removal in some situations.

Some hunters and other armed people are prepared to kill grizzlies around Yellowstone, especially during elk-hunting season. But in a large park like Katmai, the Brooks River habituated bears are far from armed people and are neither food limited nor extraordinarily hungry, so they have not been observed aggressively approaching people for food. With no surprise encounters with people, there have been no dead bears.

Does this situation apply to BC's coastal grizzlies? It depends on whether the visitors are being led by a certified guide or if they are in areas where the bears have experienced people in a consistently protected setting. If bears are approached quietly and have had some benign experiences with people, despite being shot at during the hunting season, they can be part of a viewing program. Where the bear population depends crucially on summer and fall salmon runs, the essential productivity of dense populations requires access to streams with abundant salmon. So, common sense dictates that intrusions preventing this access will have negative outcomes.

In a 1992 paper, Mattson, a renowned expert on Yellowstone grizzly behavior and ecology, tells how ravenous bears, when habituated to people, proceeded to food conditioning and became threats to visitors. Eventually, these bears were euthanized by rangers or transported to zoos—either way, they were lost to the population. To repeat, this type of mortality in Yellowstone's grizzlies is not relevant to the Pacific coastal situation. Mattson's explanation makes sense, because the Yellowstone bears, like mountain bears in Banff, Jasper, Waterton, and Glacier national parks, are nutritionally stressed. This level of food stress is not seen in bears in Katmai National Park, Kodiak National Wildlife Refuge, Anan Wildlife Observatory near Wrangell, or the Chilkoot River near Haines, Alaska, where the bears all feed on salmon. Nor is food stress occurring in bears in Knight Inlet, BC, so food conditioning and increased mortality is not a problem.

21

Hunting the Great Bear: The Crossroads of Biology, Ethics, and Management

Bears are a public heritage managed as a public trust. Like other wildlife, they legally belong to all citizens. Any species can have protected status, like bald eagles and swans, or be hunted, depending on what values people assign to them. No species evokes as much fear, respect, admiration, or conflict as the grizzly bear. When it comes to killing them, a blizzard of emotional arguments is elicited. An unbiased biologist could present arguments supporting both sides. But when it comes to grizzlies, I cannot be a fence-sitter. Since traditions of hunting grizzlies are still strong, it is worth considering where science ends and values enter. Values can change rapidly, as witnessed when hunting gorillas became unacceptable in the 1960s and then unthinkable as their numbers dwindled. A change from public acceptance of grizzly bear hunting to complete protection happened so rapidly in BC that parts of this chapter had to be changed to reflect new provincial laws. More on this later.

Making a reasoned case against hunting bears can be a daunting challenge. Few authors attempt to blend the best science, traditional values, and ethics needed. It is not surprising that people who observe and photograph bears want them protected. Being mauled by a Yellowstone grizzly is hardly a rational basis for devoting a good part of my life to championing their conservation. Having taught animal behavior and wildlife management, I understand the customary arguments supporting sport hunting of bears. In short form, a long-established biological rationale rests on demonstrating that the population is productive enough for a surplus to be hunted. In some jurisdictions, this justification is unacceptable to a majority of citizens.

For an example of the dominant place of values, in the 1980s state biologists in Utah proposed a hunting season on Sandhill cranes and reasoned there was no "biological argument" against selling permits as long as the populations remained stable. The same argument could be made for a sport hunt of bald eagles or bottle-nosed dolphins, though this is unlikely, because a government decision to hunt a species in the game management model involves concern for ethical behavior in hunters and not wasting the "game meat." That is, unless your position is that all sport hunting is wrong, not a topic grappled with here.

Hunting of waterfowl and "big game" in North America has a long tradition, dating back to obtaining food for explorers and settlers. Without getting into the weeds of the North American model of wildlife management, a successful system, suffice to say that it replaced destructive market hunting, wherein any and all species were killed and sold, a practice that led to the near extinction of species like pronghorn, bison, and elk. The scientific basis for maintaining populations of wild animals for sport and consumption is taught in ecology and wildlife management courses in our best universities. So, why not hunt grizzly bears when their numbers are not threatened? An answer involves many differences in the biology, behavior, and ecology of bears, including the awareness and appreciation that resulted from observing grizzlies up close—sustainable, non-consumptive experiences that people could only have with grizzlies that were not hunted.

Traditional bear hunting may be doomed. What are the issues? Biologists who gained degrees in wildlife science were taught that hunting or "harvesting" a species was acceptable, if a surplus was reliably demonstrated. In other words, if a segment of the public wanted to hunt them, government biologists prepared plans to manage them. This was called the "biological justification." Almost never did agency biologists tackle the ethical questions that interest the greater society. Even traditionally hunted animals, like deer or elk, were viewed by many people, not just animal rights advocates, as needing total protection, with people arguing that we already have a surplus of food. On the red-hot end of the scale are grizzly bears, perhaps close to gorilla or elephants as unacceptable targets. So, what are the differences?

When people spent time on the ground near bears and got to know individuals, a very different attitude toward them developed. Excluded, perhaps, were population biologists who followed bears after capturing, drugging, and placing radio collars on them. These nerve-wracking contacts were frequently with aggravated and aggressive bears, hardly experiences that fostered empathy for the complexity of bear temperament. In addition, trappers had little or no opportunity to study behavior for hours at a time, as animal behaviorists did. The anthropological approach to bear life helped build respect and deeper attachment. Ethologists shared trails with a creature hammered in the evolutionary forge of the ice age. Walking streams and hanging out in tree platforms to fill check-sheets with their daily goings-on developed understanding and appreciation. These experiences led me to abandon the set of values based on "renewable resources," common to my academic and wildlife colleagues who teach management of fish, waterfowl, and deer, for example. I saw bear hunting as a relict tradition, one that attracted fewer and fewer people. Even among a majority of deer, elk, and moose hunters there was little support for grizzly bear hunting, perhaps due to worries about further inroads against hunting by animal rights groups. Even if bear hunting maintained its ethical standards and "fair chase" roots, which it did not, I have yet to hear an acceptable defense of "sport hunting" of bears. To see why, take a field trip with me.

While surveying coastal BC inlets and rivers by sailboat, rigid-hulled inflatable boats, and canoes for two summers while searching for signs of grizzly abundance, I was exposed to grizzly hunting dialed up to modern style. Decades ago, hunters signed up for two- or three-week wilderness expeditions. This was a rarity among current guided hunts, as described vividly by Doug and Andrea Peacock in *The Essential Grizzly*. Coastal BC hunts had all the trappings of upscale, jet-age tourism, replete with the latest high-tech hunting gear. Here was a sample of what grizzlies were up against there.

The expedition began with the hunters and their gear being delivered by float plane to a remote tide-water logging road. The hunters were met by a licensed guide-outfitter with a tired truck just able to get the party to a rickety tree platform overlooking a stretch of salmon-spawning stream. Prior to the hunter's arrival, the guide would have scouted the site and looked for a big male or other "trophy-sized" bear. (That wish for size did not match the province's statistics on ages of bears killed, which showed lots of small bears taken, even cubs.) The goal of an expensive bear hunt was to return with a trophy. What were the ethics of hunting an animal one had no intention of eating, meanwhile parting with over $25,000 for permits, guides, and travel?

The ethical standard of "fair chase" was hardly met when a far-off bear was ambushed on a salmon stream. This scenario had the unsuspecting bear staked out like a garbage-baited bear and shot from such a distance that the bear had no chance to sense the presence of the hunter and avoid him using its superior smell, sight, and hearing. Long stalks are the essence of elk or deer hunting. But the grizzly was hunted differently, especially with big dollars chasing a promise of a sure kill. Like it or not, this idea of a near guarantee came with modern hunting, brought on by competition and money over ethics of some guided "sports." A person can appreciate why so many hunters have given up the sport, whether it is the crowds, the risk of being shot by a numbskull, or just plain discouragement by the decline in ethical standards.

To appreciate what has happened to hunting (at least the kind banned on the BC coast), a look at the entire package was required. Besides the technology and vehicles used to reach a hunting camp, gun technology and other gear have advanced tremendously. Modern bear hunting was not done with the 1804 Pennsylvania rifles and black powder used by the Lewis and Clark expedition. Although the best of their day, those weapons still required about sixty seconds to reload and lacked range and accuracy. Current hunters don't hunt bears that way unless they want to risk being counter-attacked and killed by their quarry. No chance of that with today's semi-automatic rifles with telescopic sights and the ballistics and accuracy to kill a bear at three hundred yards. To the bear, stuck with his Stone Age skills and senses, this means wounding or death from a bullet coming from the distant landscape. To the hunter, the risk of a defensive attack by a wounded and angry bear is about zero. This only happens when a bear is surprised by a hunter at close range, not when a grizzly is shot while it feeds on salmon, where sounds are masked by rushing water.

The gold standard established for professional management of a hunted species requires science-based knowledge of the species numbers and reproductive productivity to set hunting limits. Biologists have agreed to an imperative of government managers monitoring hunters and enforcing regulations. For BC, noted bear ecologist Dr. Brian Horejsi and others have shown that adequate studies to determine hunting seasons for grizzlies do not exist. Furthermore, BC has about one tenth the enforcement capability compared to Alaska, according to Horejsi's analysis. Enforcement was found to be especially inadequate in remote coastal areas, where huge, fat bears attract foreign and resident hunters. Under these conditions, a hunter can abandon a dead grizzly when he sees how small it is and pay the guide to try again. In weeks walking roads and bear trails on the coast, I discovered a dead bear on a road, shot and abandoned. Since the biological basis and public sentiment for a hunting season was not there, the hunt was terminated in 2017. Still the political pressure to keep harvesting followed the same scenario as cod management: the "harvesters"—fishermen, bear hunters, and outfitters—lobbied for more permits in the face of scientific evidence of a population decline.

As top carnivores, bears exist at low densities, compared to deer. As large animals, they require a large amount of food in absolute terms, which is usually not readily available, so they feed most of the day. That is not the case for bears that had access to streams with different species of salmon that migrate upstream through summer and fall. If grizzlies are hunted where they feed on salmon, they are being punished or killed for "coming to the kitchen." This is like ambushing antelope at a water hole in Africa, very unsportsmanlike, because no fair chase is involved. When mammals are continually threatened or harassed at one place, they learn to avoid that location. Sensible management prohibits such ambushing by hunters, because when crucial habitat components are rendered unavailable (water or rich food sources), the population declines. Where habitat security is low, food cannot be accessed due to the animals' unwillingness to take risks. Better to leave with an empty belly and survive another day than to risk death for a meal.

These considerations have special application to grizzly bears, which have low reproductive rates and exist at low densities. This life history characteristic means that every bear population does not always produce an excess of individuals, unlike rabbits and deer, so there are fewer or no surplus individuals to hunt. Therefore, grizzlies do not fit the standard model for managing deer, elk, or waterfowl. Furthermore, grizzlies live a long time, some reaching thirty years of age, a rare but classic "trophy" grizzly. But there are extremely few of them. So, what does this mean for the "trophy" in the argument for hunting grizzlies? It means that a fantasy has been promulgated, according to statistics on weights of grizzlies shot in BC and Alaska.

But there is also the avoidance issue, as with the waterhole example. In BC, consider that places where grizzlies were shot from a rough tree platform overlooked a salmon-spawning channel. When bears detect a lethal threat, they avoid that low-security habitat. As a consequence, individuals may survive, but they are driven away from an important food source, which has a cost in weight gain and in females translates in lower weight and fewer offspring. If hunting is intense, then the population will be on its way to collapse. Some individuals may opt for feeding on berries in place of salmon. This occurs in the ABC archipelago in Southeast Alaska. A small number of collared grizzlies never came down to the salmon stream but remained in the alpine zone. Modelling their productivity shows that they are smaller, like tundra grizzlies, and exist at low densities with equally low production of cubs. That contrasts with the dense protected populations of grizzlies in national parks like Katmai, where the bears get relatively undisturbed access to salmon over four to five months each year and grow to prodigious sizes. The formerly hunted populations along the BC coast had ample salmon, but numbers were depressed. Being marginal in density and numbers, they did not support much hunting, especially of large bears. What happens when hunting is replaced by lucrative bear viewing in BC? This gets us into the economics of sharing the bear "resource," as presented in the next chapter.

If you're willing to consider a middle ground, a science-based compromise between hunting everywhere and an end to all grizzly hunting, an alternative exists. It requires that government bear managers and bear-hunting advocates get more connected with bear population science—what fundamental factors drive good production of grizzly bear populations. This is bear ecology. Let's leave aside for a moment the important questions of human ethical values or personal choices about whether grizzly bears should be sport hunted. Just looking at the science, when a society's goal is providing for wildlife viewing and more grizzlies to hunt, both groups should promote complete protection of grizzlies where they concentrate to feed. Salmon streams are the factories that produce bears. Sure, bears' diets include hundreds of kinds of berries and other plants as well almost any animal, dead or alive. But the volume of fish in streams is so massive, when all five species of salmon are counted, that it makes the difference between huge coastal bears at fifty times the density of bears that don't get a crack at salmon. Coastal Katmai bears have the largest number of animals per square kilometer ever reported, according to the work by Dr. Sterling Miller and his colleagues on radio-collared animals following the Exxon oil spill. An even denser population, I suspect, is the inland bear aggregation that comes to Brooks River, due to their four months of feeding on sockeye salmon, big size, and high density. This why independent scientists have recommended a full protection strategy for salmon bears. Regrettably, protection has been resisted or rejected, perhaps suspected as the thin edge of the wedge to eliminate hunting. Maybe we should not be surprised: the state of Alaska responded with a regulation that demanded "no net loss of habitat where bears are hunted." This seems to be a reaction to advocacy by conservationists, who pressed for more protected areas, a tactic with good scientific backing. The case was made earlier against killing animals at water holes or concentrated feeding areas. These are the "kitchens" that maintain the productivity of populations. If they are protected, the animals there will produce more offspring, and the areas become population sources that provide emigrants to other areas (i.e., hunted areas), where bear mortality creates a "sink" population. To say this another way, the hunted areas kill more animals that the habitat can support, and the rich source habitat produces the emigrants. This source-sink effect has been demonstrated dramatically in Alaska's McNeil River State Wildlife Refuge, the oldest, most popular place to observe and photograph huge grizzly bears at close range. With only ten people permitted to visit the falls area at a time, the bears noticed the protection and increased in proportion to the wealth of dog salmon flooding the drainage.

Now we should circle back to who owns the bears. They are managed by the government for the enjoyment of people. That surely means all people, not just the ones who shoot the bears and hang their skins on a wall. It was reasonable to question whether a small fraction of the public should get hunting rights to all the bears over all the land and thus influence the experiences of the majority of the public or even those who will never see a bear but want them left to live their lives. There was an explosion of public interest to photograph and view bears in western Canada and Alaska. This was demonstrated by the number of television specials that featured large mammals. Studies of tourists' willingness to pay to see various wildlife species in Alaska give the prize to grizzly bears, hands down, about twice the value of seeing a wolf or a moose. This interest is reflected on the BC coast, where ecotourism on land and by boat supports about sixty businesses, which have sprung up in the last two to three decades. In the 1990s in Knight Inlet, the bears increased from under ten to a density of four or five times that number by 2016. With protection, grizzlies rapidly habituated, ignoring the presence of observers, boats, and aircraft. With full access to fat pink salmon, they became so dense that visitors could count on seeing one at any time, day or night.

22

Wild Bears or Industrial-Strength Tourism?

From National Parks to Amusement Parks

In 1832, a plan sprang from George Catlin's desire to preserve fading Indian cultures and to set aside wild land for public enjoyment and appreciation. He witnessed the onslaught of changes brought on by railroads, armed settlers, and gold seekers and predicted the rapid disappearance of native cultures. He witnessed other sites, like Niagara Falls, which had lost its natural state to commercial development. Preservation of western treasures for the public was recognized by foresighted founders. The Organic Act grew from Catlin's sentiments and proposal. Preservation of the geysers in Yellowstone would also have preserved large areas for aboriginal cultures as well as the flora and fauna—what we think of today as a large ecosystem. Another motivation was to defend the wilderness against the onslaught of gold-mining ventures, railroads, and settlements.

The creation of national parks has been hailed as one of America's best ideas. Parks protected wildlife from market hunters and ushered in 150 years of motorized visitation by rail and car and provide overnight accommodation. However, current maladies in national parks range from traffic jams due to bear watching, feeding near roads, lack of secure habitat, and reduced foods sources, which amount to real pressure for bears' survival. Wild grizzlies need wild land, lots of it. What would our parks be like with no wild bears?

Catlin never imagined how planes, trains, and automobiles could deliver so many people to wild country. Visitation to see bears in natural settings has skyrocketed. Some park managers celebrate such records, but the negative effects on grizzlies and black bears are everywhere and never beneficial. Only a new paradigm in park management can restore the possibility of survival of true wilderness nature.

Any discussion of access to national parks finds its roots in the Organic Act's dual and contradictory mandate of resource protection and public enjoyment, a mandate that was no longer in balance. Park policies and management were failing our wildlife, as I saw it. Parks had disproportionately favored motorized access and accommodated a blitz of visitation, domestic and international. Some form of control of visitors and vehicles was required to protect parks.

In Yellowstone, unlimited visitor entry and car traffic degraded the experience for people and disturbed bear access to important foods. Likewise, in Katmai's Brooks Camp, bear-viewing visitors disembarked from beached aircraft, dropped onto the same trails that bears used to get to their salmon.

Grizzly bears and people on salmon streams had been safe and compatible—the bears catching salmon and the people thrilled by seeing wild bears up close. When quiet and respectful people are nearby, mother bears have left their cubs near people, because people represent security from other bears. Females do not have to worry about aggressive adult male bears, because they avoid people. They left their cubs near people, so they were free to chase fish in swiftly flowing streams.

Bear viewing by naïve, unprepared tourists in parks was risky. Park employees also increased risks by cavalier disposal of unsecured garbage, which resulted in food-conditioned bears. Yellowstone gave us an unfortunate example of what happens when visitors and park rangers are slack on garbage management. Photographers pressed bears to capture images of bears up close, risking injury to themselves and interfering with the bears' natural attempts to move around. Examples abounded along roads in Yellowstone, where people with cameras ran to get in front of a bear that attempted to cross a road. This blocking scenario upset a female with a young cub and risked injury if she lashed out at a thoughtless or narcissistic person. Bear jams were tallied in the thousands from May to October and often overwhelmed rangers and their volunteer assistants. I watched one grizzly and her cub as they navigated four lanes of parked cars and more people streamed out of buses—tourists with no understanding of English. The time had passed to end stopping anywhere on highways to view wildlife. Even with parking and pullouts, the excitement to run for a photo placed people and cars in conflict, as injury statistics showed.

Brooks Camp devolved from a long-occupied site for aboriginal fish drying, followed by fisheries research in the mid 1900s, and then as a spectacular fly-fishing destination when air access improved. By the early 1980s, lodges accommodated overnight visitors, and others camped nearby. Daily guests came by air taxi to see bears, which replaced fishing as the prime attraction. Unfortunately, the earliest cabins and tents were placed close to the river, right where bears crossed from their beach trail to the river. The camp was situated right between the river and Naknek Lake. At that time, fewer bears came through, so there seemed little need to choose another site. Over time, cabins and lodges increased, guest facilities expanded, and a visitor center was added.

In 1967, a park bear biologist reported that Brooks Camp was situated in prime bear habitat and recommended removal. Every study since has confirmed the importance of the area for bears going to their fishing sites. Rangers reported that human-bear encounters had escalated. When my students and I reported on the number of encounters, the NPS listened and began developing plans to remove the facilities on the north side, which left one side of the river free of people. This approach also protected the rich trove of native artifacts and burial grounds around and under Brooks Camp. The development concept plan and EIS, which required twenty years of preparation, recommended a high-level vehicle bridge and transfer of the entire camp to the south side of the river.

In 2016, Brooks River had fourteen thousand visitors per year, ten thousand of them on fly-in day trips. In summer, up to twenty airplanes parked on the shore of Naknek Lake, which blocked bear access to the river. Up to seventy bears roamed the river and made bear-human conflicts inevitable and riskier. Crowds of people deterred shy bears from accessing crucial food. If another collapse or delay of the salmon migration occurred, it would create the largest aggregation of hungry bears among throngs of people ever experienced by the park service. In 1973, the run failed. Damage and injuries by aggressive bears followed. Records show that from 1965–1981, seven bears were destroyed, and eighteen were relocated away from the river. This was in a period when only fifteen or so bears used the river in July. Are bear managers prepared for the chaos to come? Yellowstone National Park experienced a food failure when they closed all the garbage dumps. Hungry, aggressive bears entered campgrounds at night. Over 220 grizzlies were killed or removed in 3 years, some by rangers, others illegally and legally outside the park. Katmai may suffer a collapse of salmon due to higher temperatures in spawning streams brought on by climate change. What will happen then?

Manage Bears or People?

Just as bear and visitor numbers peaked at Brooks Camp, the salmon numbers were also well above average. But this happy increase in bears and fish was fragile despite remarkable, burgeoning fish runs in the Naknek watershed. The history of salmon runs on the west coast is characterized by high variation. Collapse in salmon abundance is common.

Fisheries biologists have predicted warming streams with temperatures rising faster the farther north one goes. Salmon require cold water, especially in spawning tributaries, which will be hit the hardest. Drought has also reduced the volume of cool water in streams, so fish may die across broad landscapes.

When only a few salmon came late into Brooks River in 1973, all hell broke loose, as bears headed for buildings. Nothing defines a bear like its quest for food. Relationships that are going well with satiated bears are lost with food-stressed bears. The tolerant behavior of a fish-stuffed grizzly is replaced with a single-mindedness to use brute force to get food. Managers might as well forget their management guidelines for hazing "rogue" bears. All bears without enough salmon morph into rogue bears. The term "rogue" is inappropriate, because it suggests abnormal behavior—an aggressiveness that labels the bear as a sociopath among the good guys. This labeling has no scientific support. Bears have been transformed into victims when trained by misguided people. The expression "rogue human" may fit better, because such people are outliers, behaving badly toward bears.

The strained relations between the park service and its concessioner surrounding bear problems at Brooks River is described in a recent book, *At the Heart of Katmai: An Administrative History of the Brooks River Area, with Special Emphasis on Bear Management in Katmai National Park and Preserve 1912–2006*. Food conditioning of bears in camp stemmed from concessioner employees failing to follow guidelines for garbage handing. Even direct feeding of bears for photography occurred. This created bears that are both habituated to people and food-conditioned, which presaged their demise. Without compliance by employees, a late season for salmon would bring about a crisis, in public relations at least, if not damage and injuries. Visualizing seventy hungry bears marauding around cabins searching for food harkens back to the post-dump era in Yellowstone or Yosemite's car-trashing black bear crisis. In both instances, a failure to understand bear behavior and act in time led to hundreds of bears being killed when the parks believed the bears posed too great a threat of damage or injury (envision lawyers and tort cases). Whenever grizzly behavior is modified by human behavior in ways that became unacceptable, the bears always pay. But the bears that survive are also changed in ways that we little understand.

At the root of the Brooks River bear-human issues was the incompatibility of people and buildings overlapping a bear traffic zone. The Organic Act instructed parks to permit natural processes to evolve and wildlife not to be irreparably changed for future generations. To achieve this, at least one side of Brooks River should be free of people. When bears threaten people with injury or damage to property, the NPS has felt justified to kill bears. All the evidence suggests that the killing could have been avoided if enforcement of rules prevented food-conditioning of bears. Killing Brooks bears can also be avoided, but it will require limiting the number of people and better separation of people and bears. When park HQ is unable to resist lobbying and congressional meddling for the benefit of private interests, then rangers will be faced with destruction of a wildlife icon, admired and nearly worshipped by the public.

A central fact remains: the camp sits on trails that the bears have used for thousands of years. More elevated platforms and construction of a ten-foot-high bridge may separate bears and people near the river. However, the bridge (with an eight-foot-wide vehicle deck) will still disgorge trucks and seven to eight hundred people per day in places used by bears at all times on their way to fish. Lost among all the justifications for this gargantuan bridge are these facts: all overnight accommodation, a restaurant and bar, a park service complex, and trails between all these are situated on top of paths that bears have used for ages. As visitation has increased, people have had to weave around one of seventy bears without guides or leaders. This creates a radical management situation, far more permissive and less enforced than any other bear-viewing location, whether government run or private.

Climate change magnifies the scale of a potential calamity. Loss of salmon will render the hazing techniques currently employed ineffective and potentially dangerous. Large bears made aggressive from hunger are known to defend a resource. Having a bear charge among people is no place to use a gun. Even if a clear shot were possible, a wounded bear is a nightmare come to life. Even tranquilizing a large bear takes time for complete immobilization. With so much water around, a groggy bear could easily drown in the river or lake.

Re-wilding Brooks River and Bears

Until the NPS abides by its legal mandate to protect cultural and biological resources, alternative plans are needed to meet the protection clause without treading on the enjoyment portion. Are there options for viewing bears while reducing impacts from people?

One obvious option to relieve stress on bears and avoid crises it to limit visitation to day trips. Bears gain access to salmon at night and early morning, especially shy or aggressive bears. Overnight accommodations for visitors can be built at Lake Camp, where the Naknek River flows into Naknek Lake. The NPS has docks and other facilities there at the end of the road from King Salmon. Wilderness campsites are available on bear-free islands. Considering weather limitations to flying and to avoid aircraft parked where bears walk, boat-based transport to Brooks could link the twenty-mile gap. By using jet drives, a larger vessel with shallow draft could navigate the Naknek River all the way to King Salmon. Fuel consumption and trip costs can be reduced if high-speed catamarans or even newer battery-based propulsion systems are employed. Day visitors can be returned to overnight accommodations, restaurants, and bars well away from bear country.

In 2012, Katmai established five video cameras that live-streamed bear activity and attracted viewers from around the world. In 2015, about six million hours were tallied by people watching bears and other wildlife. Fifty thousand comments were racked up in one week. Not only can many more people view bears than can physically visit Brooks Camp, many people, including rangers, can learn about bears from a distance.

More efficient transportation reduces fuel consumption, pollution, and climate change, a growing impact of adventure tourism to distant and exotic places. Yes, watching live animal behavior on a screen hardly compares with being there in person, but we know that the quality and uniqueness of professional wildlife television specials assures that viewers witness fascinating behavior that is almost never seen on individual excursions. There will still be many opportunities to observe grizzly bears in the wild, but rare locations, so essential to the ecological processes that Brooks River represents, will be protected and allowed to function and evolve undisturbed. For a similar example of complete protection, consider the caves of Chauvet and Lascaux when, in 1963 France, excluded visitors from entering the caves. The wall art was being damaged by carbon dioxide, heat, and humidity.

Brooks Camp's aging structures require replacement. Visitors have expressed dissatisfaction with the age, price, and cleanliness of cabins, factors which make a move timely. Replacement of the lodge or adding structures risks destruction of priceless archeological resources found everywhere under Brooks Camp. Further expansion to meet increasing demand requires digging trenches for sewer, water, and electrical infrastructure, raising the same problems for cultural artifact losses and more disturbance of bears.

23

Bears Are Like Us: Restoring Their Future

If grizzly bears are going to have a future beyond token representation in a few wild places, their wild homes require restoration. Their need for wilderness aligns with ours. The current pandering for collaboration among private stakeholders only provides "wins" for current users and special interests. Are the interests of future Americans, the wildlife, and wilderness habitat winning?

First, we should confront wrong-headed language like "natural resources," which labels and treats remaining wildlife and natural forests as economic commodities instead of reservoirs of beauty, solitude, and quiet values. Wildlife management has become game farming, while national parks policy gurus have acquiesced to intrusive recreation, such as commercial rafting and mountain biking, and failed to protect wildness and wildlife. "Resources" is a vague, outdated concept flowing from another mind swindler, "multiple use," a term that subsumes and satisfies our addiction for giving a little something of economic value to everyone. Multiple-use thinking remains deep in the organizational culture of the US Forest Service (USFS) and the Bureau of Land

Management (BLM), both of which have, ironically, tolerated single-use dominance everywhere, especially by logging companies and livestock ranchers, above all other interests. That western tradition left landscapes denuded of tallgrasses, trout, sage grouse, elk, and grizzlies. Streams became polluted everywhere when ranchers gained influence. Private exploitation of public land led inevitably to less wild land per person with depleted wildlife populations and a landscape with an end point that resembled much of wilderness-depleted Europe.

Many opportunities remain for restoring wildness in our national parks and forests, if only governments adhere to legal mandates, currently subverted by special interests and their political minions. At the top of the list in national parks is action to move accommodations and facilities in parks to gateway towns outside parks. This has been accomplished in the Sierra Nevada Mountain Range, but failures abound, like the expansion of developments around Brooks River in Katmai National Park. Suitable land is available at the entrance to Katmai, and native organizations are on board with that option. A massive bridge and boardwalk over Brooks River portend a repetition of the 1980s Fishing Bridge fiasco in Yellowstone. Political interference on behalf of tourism businesses sank the relocation effort of Grant Village. There are now two major developments on critical grizzly bear habitat, instead of one.

Grand Teton and Yellowstone National Parks could also reduce threats to grizzly bears on their borders by negotiating protective buffer zones with state governments. Instead of opening a hunting season on the park bears when they move outside park boundaries, they need special protection, starting with road and trail closures.

An example from wolf studies in Alaska's Denali National Park is instructive. In a conversation years ago with Al Lovaas, a research biologist there, I learned that every wolf pack in the park was exposed to trapping, because all wolf packs ranged beyond park boundaries. So much for our national parks' reputation for protecting the nation's most admired and valued large carnivores. Grizzly bears suffer the same syndrome. Bears and wolves are targeted by hunters, who believe that killing predators provides more moose, deer, elk, and caribou, although no science supports that thinking. Even if true, a majority of Americans do not support government programs in western states or Alaska that reduce the numbers of carnivores.

National parks have numerous examples of slack enforcement or outright mismanagement that regional directors can easily remedy. The proliferation of tour buses in Yellowstone should require certified guides on board with the language and skills to prevent tourists from rushing toward grizzly bears, a regular occurrence along highways. Reducing speed limits and better enforcement would reduce the slaughter of wildlife on roads.

In Alaskan parks, moving swiftly on squatters' camps in remote locations would benefit bears. People produce garbage that is attractive to bears, and when the bears become intolerant, people are killed, as happened to Timothy Treadwell. Each violator should be removed immediately and fined for harassing bears. Visitors who behave like commercial photographers should be denied entry to parks when caught violating rules for approaching animals. These rogue photographers became so competitive and uncooperative at McNeil Falls in the early 1970s that my friend, Alaskan author/photographer Tom Walker, took them to task for harassing bears.

Privatizing Profits, Socializing Costs: Concessions in Our National Parks

In July 1985, a big brown bear walked right in front of me on the main trail through Brooks Camp. Hal Grovert, an experienced park ranger, was armed with a shotgun loaded with rubber slugs. He fired one at the bear's rump, hoping to convince it to move along and not use camp trails, but the bear immediately reversed toward us when hit. I guessed that the bear thought it was being punished for going the wrong way, quite different from Hal's interpretation. Seeing us, the bear diverted, just like any of the hundreds of bears encountering people near Brooks River in Katmai National Park.

Escalating bear-human conflicts are a direct result of the Brooks Camp expansion from a tiny row of tents in 1950 to an expanded complex of fifty-five buildings in the middle of prime habitat for seventy plus bears. The housing, ranger station, maintenance shops, power plants, and visitor facilities also overlap with priceless archeological gems, sites sacred to indigenous people and their descendants. For two decades beginning in 1986, the park spent a good portion of its budgets preparing a development concept plan followed by a formal environmental impact statement (EIS), which received public support. As described earlier, the preferred plan was to move the camp well away from prime habitat and across the river, leaving the north side to the bears, where many trails connected the beach trail to the salmon in Brooks River. It would meet the needs of bears and people well into the future. The ten-year plan hit a wall when, as I covered earlier, Senator Lisa Murkowski was asked by commercial stakeholders to intervene and lean on the Secretary of the Interior, Sally Jewell. The park was cajoled into reneging on relocating the camp, agreeing only to move park staff housing. The result was a larger degradation of habitat, continued conflicts with bears, and further crowding in a serene gem in this remote Alaskan wilderness.

Rather than doing a supplemental environmental impact statement (a standard practice when an EIS is challenging), the park's regional office orchestrated a "review" of bear management. Astonishingly, this consisted largely of interviews with the conflicted lodge and maintenance staff. Then the office released recommendations for changes. That report acknowledged people with no credibility about bear behavior. The superintendent and his staff made no attempt to contact the primary investigator of the original science or former students who had reviewed past research and all but ignored their own wildlife biologist, Tamara Olson, the person most knowledgeable about the impacts of various plans. The final justification for the bridge and keeping the camp in place were trivial improvements in visitor access and unobstructed bear and fish movement on the river. Regrettably, this stealth capitulation was another symptom of mismanagement and violation of the Organic Act ("to preserve nature unimpaired"), because private business owners were expanding their operations, given the no-limits edicts in the heart of this spectacular wilderness park. At the National Park Service's discretion, it ignored congressional instructions to move facilities and visitor accommodations to gateway communities outside park boundaries.

In 2016 I joined Jack Hession, a long-time leader and powerhouse with the Sierra Club, to approach Earthjustice lawyers in Anchorage with a detailed report that I had prepared with Ray Bane, a former superintendent of Katmai. We hoped it would receive legal support under the National Environmental Protection Act (NEPA) or the Organic Act to require the NPS to redo their EIS or initiate a supplemental EIS in view of the radical changes in the relocation plans. The lawyers concluded that an intervention by a judge was unlikely. Next, we appealed to the director of the Alaska chapter of National Parks Conservation Association (NPCA) in Anchorage. We had no better luck with the new director than the former one, who collaborated closely with top park administrators. For me the Kool-Aid had been passed around the table for the Bridge Too Far. My faith in the legitimacy of the federal government's ability to abide by federal law dropped another notch when an organization of park service retirees took a pass on this issue too.

Unless a way was found to alert and engage a broader public to contact and shame the National Park Service and the caucus of senators, these travesties of corporate dominance over conservation would continue, especially in an era of libertarian ideology and suppression of the best scientific information. Even the liberal elite seemed happy to make excuses and justify expensive trips to exotic wild places as support for the dwindling islands of diversity. I knew this, because I have been not only part of ecotourism guiding but also a big defender. I was drawn to grizzly bears not as a "bear witch" (doing well by doing good) or as an animal rights advocate but because I wanted to speak up for grizzly bears. They are the ultimate vote-less visible minority, a test for our materialist culture to show some restraint. Currently, our behavior toward Mother Earth amounts to blaspheming the contributions of wilderness advocates and previous politicians with principles who had passed laws that we should be proudly explaining to our grandchildren.

Federal park leaders should be recognized when they reach out to universities to fund independent research. Park managers who fail to apply "best practices" based on science, such as that contained in the EIS for Brooks Camp, waste millions of dollars and also degrade the park. The massive bridge and elevated walkway under construction at remote Brooks Camp in Katmai National Park is a flagrant example. If science was meant to contribute, then how could studies carried out under contract by independent researchers and their own biologists be ignored when Katmai administrators spun on a dime in response to pressure from Alaskan senators and edicts from the Department of the Interior? Solving the crowding problem by constructing an over-engineered bridge and boardwalk fails the bear protection smell test. Conservation was ignored in a surrender to industrial-strength tourism.

Alaska's senators led the charge for the tourism business when it came to bullying the feds in Alaska and park personnel when they try to protect wildlife. First, it was the late Ted Stevens, who threatened to cut park service budgets if visitor limits were imposed, no matter how bad the crowding or how deafening the aircraft noise. When the regional director moved ahead with plans for the relocation of Brooks Camp in Katmai National Park, he was complying with the mandate of the National Parks Organic Act, which requires parks to conserve resources unimpaired. Senator Murkowski ended that. To accommodate over five hundred people per day arriving and departing in floatplanes, Brooks turned into a theme park, where visitors waited in line for a short visit on elevated platforms to shout and clap when bears caught salmon leaping over Brooks Falls.

Who will manage the perfect storm when the salmon run collapses and hungry, aggressive bears rain chaos on naïve visitors sleeping among dozens of active bear trails? Both ecological theory and on-the-ground studies predict that carnivores will take greater risks near people when starved. Is the park service prepared for tort lawsuits when starving Brooks bears come to the river?

In Anchorage, the regional office received a letter from two prominent grizzly bear experts informing them that "it is not if there will be bear injuries, but when," their assessment after seeing the current situation. I can assure the park service that I will not be giving a deposition in their favor when the charge of mismanagement is brought.

So, in 2018, we have a $7-million bridge designed to support trucks slated for construction over a tiny wild river that will join the old camp to a new one, both laid over a network of bear trails and right on top of archeological treasures and sacred native gravesites concentrated over a square kilometer of land. This fiasco awakens memories of a similar betrayal in Yellowstone to remove the decrepit Fishing Bridge facilities and build Grant Village, a plan that likewise was sabotaged by Wyoming state senators, resulting in two developments. When the National Park Service celebrated its one hundredth anniversary in August 2016, it might have honored its original mandate. Instead, at Brooks River, it chose to sacrifice national treasures on the altar of tourism and profit.

Turning Points on a Journey

After my recovery, I went back to field work to search for ways for people and grizzlies to co-exist without fear and guns. My unbelievable rescue by the West Yellowstone Hot Shot fire team and emergency medical crews had given me a second lease on life to reengage with the grizzly bear problem.

Well before I headed to Katmai, a furor had boiled up over relocation of Yellowstone's Fishing Bridge development, which sat on prime grizzly habitat. The issue was hung up on the confounded tension between wildlife protection and visitor accommodation inside parks during an era of tourism expansion. From the ramparts, I joined bear advocates as they lost out to power politics driven by gateway tourism businesses. Their senators coerced the NPS to develop Grant Village with 430 recreational vehicle sites in nearby pristine grizzly bear habitat.

At the time, I remained optimistic that better scientific information could change management and policy for better treatment of bears and their habitat. That belief energized me to begin a long series of applied behavior studies at Brooks River under a contract with Katmai National Park. However, the application of all that work hit a wall right after development plans to relocate the badly situated camp surfaced. That fiasco played out in 2017 and continues into the present.

Where does a person find even a thread of hope for grizzlies in a gun culture and more men wanting to kill one? Not among the members of the Alaska Board of Game, who made destruction of bears and wolves easier and more savage to placate moose, Dall sheep, and caribou hunters. Not among the state game departments around Yellowstone, which claimed that a hunt on bears, only barely recovered, would not endanger survival of park grizzly bears. Fortunately, in British Columbia, citizens advocated to end annual hunts, so that is a harbinger of change. Contributing to that policy decision was growth in bear-viewing businesses, mostly on the coast. The economic advantages of photography and bear watching over shooting are over-whelming. As people begin to appreciate the richness, variety, and sensitivity of grizzly behavior, it is more likely that grizzlies will be valued as the benign, dog-like ice age relics that they are.

We should not give in to the neo-environmentalists, who encourage a human-managed earth in the Anthropocene, where feral cats, starlings, cockroaches, and urban coyotes are accepted as dominants. As Theodore Roosevelt once said, "In any moment of decision, the best thing you can do is the right thing. The worst thing you can do is nothing."

Change in our embedded traditional beliefs about grizzly bears will take time, but North Americans have passed laws to protect wilderness when pressured by far-sighted citizens. Wild land is the home of grizzlies and an umbrella for other threatened animals and plants. The time for renewal of this impulse has arrived. As chimpanzees, mountain gorillas, elephants, wolves, and even sharks are studied up close and portrayed sympathetically, the perceptions of the public shift from demonization to appreciation of the social communication in their complex lives. Bloodlust and appeals to the mythic "ancient hunter" in our DNA have given way to the need to halt the global extinction of top carnivores and highly social mammals.

24

Dos and Don'ts in Grizzly Country

Preparation for an encounter with a grizzly bear begins with the right mental view and then adding perspective—taking in the sense of awareness learned from experienced bear biologists. Subduing fear or uncertainty when unfamiliar with bears is necessary but difficult. Even after all my years of bear encounters, I still have to remind myself to stay focused when in bear country. I work to avoid complacency, because every wild creature is a product of its experience, which could include negative encounters with people. Becoming accustomed to uncertainty will increase your confidence to react appropriately.

Being more alert than a bear permits a person to slowly back away while facing the bear. If it sees or smells you right off, aim your bear spray while you start small talk, explaining to the bear that you plan to back away if she will wait a bit. If the bear is standing looking at you, it is probably trying to decide whether you are a threat, so keep calm. Most likely it will turn and run. Steel yourself not to run if it charges toward you. Chances are it is testing you and will divert aside if you shout and stand your ground while releasing spray when the bear is twenty to thirty feet away.

If you are planning to hike in the backcountry, distant from roads, it is best to have companions, the more the better. National parks recommend four people, as there have been no attacks on groups of this size. Never wear earbuds. Make noise every so often to avoid a surprise close encounter. A surprised bear is an angry bear, and an angry bear is a dangerous bear. Many books have been written about how to stay safe, but few emphasize the importance of suppressing idle conversation. Constant alertness to what is far ahead will help you detect a feeding or sleeping bear.

I can stay much more aware on trails if I make a conscious mental shift by suppressing any tendency to reminisce or fantasize and become instead a primitive sensory animal, constantly scanning everything ahead, listening intently, and sniffing for wet bear or the odor of dead meat. If you anticipate a grizzly bear ahead, you will be psychologically ready when one comes into view.

In the rare case that the bear is going to contact you, the best tactic is to drop flat and protect your neck with your hands and arms. The bear may nip or bite, but an inert person does not elicit a shaking attack, as does fighting back, which is the surprised-bear scenario. Even rarer is a grizzly attack that is predatory, so fighting it off with a hiking stick or big branch is worth trying, although bear spray is still the better option, because it is painful to the eyes, nose, and mouth tissue, not to mention the choking effect when inhaled. Holding a spray weapon against an oncoming bear puts you in a defensive stance that a bear understands. This sometimes requires the steadfast courage born of combat training or its equivalent. If you are a rank novice around bears, consider hiking with others who have more experience.

You will avoid some troubles with bears by rejecting the myth that bear vision is poor. Yes, their eyes are unable to distinguish an immobile person against a patterned background, but they are excellent at detecting movements, even at considerable distances. Often a grizzly will circle an object that it wants to identify in order to get downwind to smell and identify the object with certainty. Because their sense of smell is so acute, it is their confirmatory sense, whereas vision tells them something is out there that needs closer attention. Bears can detect extremely low concentrations of odors. Believe me—you smell a lot stronger to a bear than you think you do.

A bear's odor detection is so efficient that wind direction can be a significant safety issue. You can surprise a bear more often at short range if the wind is blowing from her to you. Your best plan is to let a bear detect you far outside its personal space. Again, my experience says the bear wants to keep as clear of you as you do of it.

I have emphasized the differences in the behavior of grizzlies toward people in different places. The short message is that protected grizzlies, including mothers with cubs, around salmon streams that have had prolonged contact with people are least likely to be aggressive. However, mountain grizzlies are generally less well nourished, have had little contact with people, and being hunted, may be the most challenging and least predictable. If you are going to be working in their habitat, many options exist to avoid conflict and injury. Further specific advice on avoiding encounters with bears when camping can be found in many books and national park handouts. The topic is beyond the scope of this book.

25

Stories Out There of a Changed Bear

Much of the mystique surrounding grizzlies may never be dispelled, and perhaps that is good, as long as we maintain a reverence for the continued existence of bears and preserve areas such as McKinley National Park in such a way that they may continue to live without harassment by man.

—Adolph Murie *The Grizzlies of Mount McKinley*

Our modern relationship with the grizzly bear reflects either an appreciation for or apathy toward nature. Is it still possible to find a path back, to watch a grizzly with wonder in untrammeled lands? What are the waypoints on this journey that guide the grizzly's future?

If we hope to slow and reverse the grizzly's slide into extinction, change is essential in our cultural tradition of domination, hatred, and apathy. Throughout this book, I have tried to show how our literature is fraught with exaggerated accounts of encounters with this animal—even benign encounters, like the misinterpretation of the clear and detailed accounts in the journals of Lewis and Clark. All three historians renowned for their editing of these journals (Gary Moulton, Elliot Coues, and Reuben Gold Thwaites) seemed to ignore the factual language about bears in their scholarly efforts to present us with unadulterated editions of the journals.

Besides the grizzly bear mythology that holds sway, we need to change the attitudes of the bear researchers on the front lines, particularly regarding their failure to recognize the effects of handling grizzly bears. Twenty years after my horrible attack, while attempting to observe bear responses to hikers on trails, I discovered how myths can dominate well-established truths, a hazard now swallowing us whole. Fortunately, our Yellowstone research approach was later adopted by bear biologist Kerry Gunther for his master's thesis shortly after my 1977 Yellowstone accident.

I also looked into a report by the Interagency Grizzly Bear Study Team, who used intrusive capturing techniques from 1979–1980. That study became the basis for a Montana State University master's thesis by Bart O. Schleyer in 1983. He was an experienced outdoorsman and expert bear trapper, employed for studies of radio-collared grizzlies by the federal agency. (This much-loved friend of many people subsequently disappeared on a hunting trip in Canada's Yukon Territory, apparently killed by a grizzly.

I had a serious reason to carefully review Schleyer's thesis, because I was engaged as a grizzly bear expert in a $3 million lawsuit involving a research grizzly that killed Roger May while camping in the Rainbow Point campground west of Yellowstone on June 24, 1983. The bear, known as Bear 15, had been captured and approached closely a number of times by Schleyer as part of a study. I discovered this bear had been captured a total of eighteen times, starting when it was a cub. Reported to be aggressive toward people by more than one observer, Schleyer wrote in his thesis (p. 109) that it kept him up a tree from about 10 p.m. to 2 a.m. and "remained in the immediate area for a few hours." This, of course, was before this bear launched a predatory attack on Roger

May and fed on him. Bear 15 was trapped and destroyed close to the attack site. So much human flesh was found in the bear's stomach that there was no question that this was the bear that preyed on Mr. May.

My motives for searching Schleyer's thesis were, first, to become informed on the history of the behavior of this grizzly for the legal firm suing the United States Forest Service and later to correct some reporting that had confused my own non-intrusive, observational study with the federal research that Schleyer was carrying out. My conclusion, based on his thesis and other documents, was that Bear 15 presented an unusual risk to visitors and campers and that it might well have been categorized as too much of a threat to people to be released back into the wild. However, that would have required the responsible agency to assess all the records on this much-handled bear.

As aggressive as this bear was toward people, it also raised the question of whether constant trapping, ear-tagging, and collaring had resulted in a man-hater syndrome, a question yet to be addressed by any grizzly bear researchers. Bear 15 had been captured in snares and culvert traps with bait, which may have not only food-conditioned and habituated him to people but also left him with a bad attitude toward humans, especially since three kinds of drugs had been used on him over the eighteen capture processes. It would have been possible to track Bear 15 as he went toward campgrounds, just like Yosemite biologists did with problem black bears. Federal biologists would have had to assess all their bears to identify the few that posed unusual risks to campers and assign staff to follow them--not a simple endeavor. The fatal attacks on people, following recovery from drugs, should also elicit more investigation into future behavior of bears that have been drugged for capture, which could encourage a change in tracking paradigms.

Regrettably, the lead government scientist at the time took a strong position that negative impacts from trapping and drugging grizzly bears had negligible behavioral and physical effects. I wrote a report, contracted through him, that said otherwise, only to learn that all ten copies of my report had vanished. That tidbit came from a Washington budget manager, who called me trying to find a copy to determine if the contract funds had supplied a product. More rigorous research on capture effects, by Marc Cattet et al. (2008), corroborated my preliminary conclusions and predictions.

Another innovative and non-intrusive method of learning about and tracking individuals is documenting direct observation, like those of Dr. Jim Halfpenny, an animal tracks expert and certified field guide. In his Naturalist's World, a teaching laboratory in Gardiner, Montana, he has laminated sheets containing mug shots and bear records over years to keep track of grizzly bear families. This pioneering technique has proven useful to promote interest and appreciation of known grizzlies as the fascinating large creatures they are.

If capturing grizzlies in Yellowstone creates aversions to people, then this disturbance would add another cause of bears moving out of the park. Handling could also make them more prone to charge if they feel threatened by people as a result of capture and handling. The jury is out on this issue. It needs to be studied in a park with many people on trails but with negligible experience with bears.

Despite my earlier effusive appreciation for Lewis and Clark's unadorned writing about wildlife, it is clear that one richly detailed account of Lewis fleeing into a river at the approach of a grizzly cannot be interpreted as a charge toward Lewis "at full speed" or viewed as an attack. When Lewis turned and faced the bear, waist deep in the river, the bear turned and ran off.

Another rarely cited source of benign interactions with grizzly bears prior to repeating firearms is Osborne Russell's *Journal of a Trapper*, which covers his nine years of wilderness experience from 1834–1843. What can we make of this account?

> In going to visit my traps a distance of 3 or 4 mils early in the morning have frequently seen 7 or 8 standing about the

> clumps of Cherry bushes on their hind legs gathering cherries with surprising dexterity not even deigning to turn their Grizzly heads to gaze at the passing trapper but merely casting a sidelong glance at him without altering their position.

North Americans trappers extirpated beavers during the fur trade, but now beavers are back, resuming their crucial role over the landscape in high-elevation watersheds. Beavers are widespread enough now to be hated and loved, similar to the grizzly, wherever they live. The same schizoid attitudes followed the alligator in Florida, a potentially dangerous large reptile with which people have learned to co-exist. With sufficient will, we can assure our grizzly friends that their habitat will be restored and maintained, despite the last vestiges of self-aggrandizement among hunters, intolerance, and ignorance.

The historical relationship of humans and bears in the American West followed parallel streams of changed behavior after encounters. Journals of the earliest explorers and trappers showed the mainly benign behavior of grizzlies toward people. Then followed a period of dominionistic values with trapping, shooting, and poisoning of all grizzly bears when sheep and cattle were introduced. Soon the grizzly reacted with defensive aggressiveness to mistreatment, resulting in loss of habitat. Only much later, when Alaskan salmon-eating grizzlies were fully protected in parks and had a surplus of food, did the bears' essential nature return to tolerance and avoidance of people. When bears treat us with relative disinterest, such as around salmon streams, we respond with protective regulations that inspire tolerance and appreciation.

A lifetime of direct experience with bears, from the Sierras to the Northern Rockies and on salmon streams from BC to the Alaskan Peninsula, left me with an appreciation for their majesty and behavioral diversity. I was able to compare their temperament and personality under widely varying management regimes and government policies, supplemented by historical research, scientific publications, and the advice and insights of specialist colleagues. One end of the temperament spectrum were salmon-satiated mothers, like those at Brooks River, who trust their tiny cubs to people as a refuge to guard against the risks of infanticidal adult male bears. At the other end, in vivid contrast, is Bear 15, a food-conditioned, often-captured outlier, who was eventually destroyed as a man-killer.

When this uniquely sentient creature is perceived as responding to us according to how we treat him, a path to survival opens up. We are at the end of a long period of attempted dominion over this apex predator, and my hope is that we can rise to the challenge of restraint and tolerance required of us.

Source Notes

Chapter 1: A Mauling and a Mountaintop Rescue

1. Case Incident Record Number: 770637, Yellowstone National Park.

Chapter 2: Rescue and Recovery

1. Jim Thompson, personal communication from the pilot of the rescue helicopter (2017).
2. Medical report from the Yellowstone Lake Hospital physician.

Chapter 3: Bears as Adversary

1. Paul Russell Cutright, *Lewis and Clark: Pioneering Naturalists,* (Urbana, IL: University of Illinois Press, 2003), 261.
2. Daniel Botkin, *Our Natural History: The Lessons of Lewis and Clark.* (Oxford: Oxford University Press, 2004).
3. Gary Moulton, ed., *The Journals of Lewis & Clark Expedition,* (Lincoln: University of Nebraska Press, 1988).
4. Ernest Thompson Seton, *Lives of Game Animals Vol. II.* (New York: The Literary Guild of America, Inc., 1937), 110.

    "The giant has become inoffensive now. He is shy, indeed, and seeks only to be let mind his own business. At the slightest hint of man in his vicinity, he will fly fast and far, and covers many mountains to be sure that he has left the dreaded taint behind. It is modern guns that has made this change of heart."

5. Hans Kruuk, "Surplus killing by carnivores," Journal of Zoology 166 (2) (February 1972): 233–246.
6. Henry Beston, *The Outermost House: A Year of Life on the Great Beach of Cape Cod,* (Boston: G. K. Hall & Co., 1861).

Chapter 4: Bears as Friends

1. Moulton, Gary, ed., *The Journals of Lewis & Clark Expedition,* (Lincoln: University of Nebraska Press, 1988), 292.

   12 June 1805, "... and having entirely forgotten to reload my rifle, a large white bear, or rather brown bear, had perceived and crept up on me within 20 steps before I discovered him; in the first moment I drew up my gun to shoot, but at the same instance recollected that she was not loaded" .... "he was then briskly advancing on me" .... "in this situation I thought of retreating in a brisk walk as fast as he was advancing" ... "I had no sooner turned myself about but he pitched at me, open mouthed and full speed, I ran about 80 yards and found he gained on me fast, I then run into the water" ... "I ran hastily into the water about waist deep, and faced about" .... "at this instance he arrived at the edge of the water within about 20 feet of me; the moment I put myself in this attitude of defense he suddenly wheeled about" ... "and retreated with quite as great precipitation as he had just before pursued me,"

2. Gretchen C. Daily, *Nature's Services: Societal Dependence on Natural Ecosystems,* (Washington, DC: Island Press, 1997), 369.

   "Deforestation, for instance, increases runoff, nutrient loss, and erosion; these effects are magnified and may carry on indefinitely when forest land is converted permanently to agriculture (Vitousek 1983)." Finally, safeguarding ecosystem services represents one of the wisest economic investments society could make."

3. National Parks Organic Act of 1916.

   "The service thus established shall promote and regulate the use of the Federal areas known as national parks, monuments, and reservations hereinafter specified by such means and measures as conform to the fundamental purposes of the said parks, monuments, and reservations, which purpose is to conserve the scenery and the natural and historic objects and the wild life therein and to provide for the enjoyment of the same in such manner and by such means as will leave them unimpaired for the enjoyment of future generations."

4. Timothy Treadwell quotes based on my personal notes from his telephone call to me in Logan, Utah, December 1993.

Chapter 5: Coming Home: The Real Bear

1. F. Fraser Darling, *A Herd of Red Deer: A Study in Animal Behaviour*, (Oxford: Oxford University Press, 1937).
2. Frederick C. Dean, *Brown Bear-Human Interrelationship Study*. (National Park Service, 1968): 126–301.
3. Will Troyer, *Movements, Behavior and Population Characteristics of Brown Bears at Brooks River*, (1980).

Chapter 6: Why Bears Attack

1. Stephen Herrero, *Bear Attacks: Their Causes and Avoidance*, (Toronto: McClelland & Stewart, 2002).
2. Frank Norris, personal communication in a letter to the author.
3. Doug Peacock, *Grizzly Years: In Search of the American Wilderness*, (New York: Henry Holt and Company, 1990).

Chapter 7: Too Much Is Never Enough

1. Ernest Thompson Seton, *Lives of Game Animals Vol. II*. (New York: The Literary Guild of America, Inc., 1937), 110.

Chapter 12: Salmon Bears Build Rainforests

1. James Faro, "McNeil River Bear Study," *Alaska Fish Tales & Game Trails* 27 (1971): 10–11.
2. Allan L. Egbert, *The Social Behavior of Brown Bears at McNeil River*, (Logan, UT: Utah State University, 1978).
3. T.L. Olson, R.C. Squibb, B.K. Gilbert, "Brown Bear Diurnal Activity and Human Use: A Comparison of Two Salmon Streams," *Ursus* 10 (International Association for Bear Research and Management, Sept. 1995): 547–555.
4. Troyer 1980; Dean 1968; Kathy Jope, Braaten, and Gilbert 1987; Warner 1987; Olson and Squibb 1991.
5. Katherine Ringsmuth, *At the Heart of Katmai: An Administrative History of the Brooks River Area, with Special Emphasis on Bear Management in Katmai National Park and Preserve 1912–2006*, (National Park Service, 2013).
6. Will Troyer, *Bear Wrangler: Memoirs of an Alaskan Pioneer Biologist*. (Fairbanks: University of Alaska Press), 2010.
7. Chauncey Juday, Rich, and Mann (1932).

Chapter 13: Rapid Evolution of Bear Behavior

1. Jonathan Weiner, *The Beak of the Finch*, (New York, Random House, 1995), a captivating account of the twenty-year study of Galapagos finch evolution by Peter and Rosemary Grant.
2. Christopher Servheen and John Schoen, "Brown Bears at Brooks Camp, Katmai National Park: Recommendations for Management," letter to Katmai superintendent, 1998.
3. Trevor D. Price, A. Qvarnström, and D. E. Irwin, "The role of phenotypic plasticity in driving genetic evolution," *Proceedings of the Royal Society Biological Science* 270, (London, 2003): 1433–1440.

4. Rachel Mazur, *Speaking of Bears: The Bear Crisis and a Tale of Rewilding from Yosemite, Sequoia, and Other National Parks.* (Guilford, CT and Helena, MT: Falcon Guides, 2015).

Chapter 14: Calculating Bears

1. Henry E. McCutchen,"Black Bear Species/Area Relationships Studies at Rocky Mountain National Park," *Park Science* 7 no.3 (Spring 1987): 19.

   "Three-quarters of a century of bear control and avoidance conditioning by park authorities has created a creature so fearful of people that its usable habitat is limited to the most inaccessible regions of the park . . . areas that account for only a small fraction of Rocky Mountain's 265.000 acres preserve."

2. Ministry of Environment, Lands and Parks, *Grizzly Bear Conservation in BC: Background Report,* (Victoria, BC: Government of British Columbia, 1995).

Chapter 15: Wild Bears, Wilder Tourists

1. Hiram Martin Chittenden, *The Yellowstone National Park: Historical and Descriptive,* (Cincinnati: The Robert Clarke Company, 1895).
2. Robert Keiter, *To Conserve Unimpaired: The Evolution of the National Parks Idea,* (Washington, DC: Island Press, 2015).

Chapter 16. Teaching Bears Bad Habits Then Punishing Them

1. Bruce Hastings, BK Gilbert, and DL Turner. 1981. Black bear behavior and human-bear relationship in Yosemite National Park, 1978-1979. Cooperative Park Studies Unit Technical Report No. 2 university of California, Davis, CA

Chapter 17. Wilderness Intact

1. Don E. Dumond.2005. A Naknek Chronicle: Ten thousand Years in a Land of Lakes and rivers and Mountains of Fire. GPO, National Park Service, Washington, DC.
2. Egbert, Allan L. 1978. The Social Behavior of Brown Bears at McNeil River. PhD Dissertation, Utah State University, Logan, Utah 1978.
3. Katherine Ringsmuth. 2013. At the Heart of Katmai: An Administrative History of the Brooks River Area, with Special Emphasis on Bear Management in Katmai National Park and Preserve 1912-2006.

Chapter 18. Science Friction

1. National Park Service. 1994. Development Concept Plan and Environmental Impact Statement: Brooks River Area. Katmai National Park and Preserve.
2. Bo Bennett. 2000. Rods and Wings: A History of the Fishing Lodge Business in Bristol Bay, Alaska. Anchorage: Publication Consultants.
3. National Park Service. 2006. Bear-Human Conflict Management Plan: Katmai National Park and Preserve, Aniakchak National Monument and Preserve, Alagnak Wild River.
4. https://www.nps.gov/katm/learn/management/upload/KATMBMP06.pdf

Chapter 19. Sacred Bears: Early Native Ties to Grizzlies

1. 1. Jack W. Brink. 2008. Imagining Head-Smashed-In: Aboriginal Buffalo Hunting on the Northern Plains. Athabasca University Press.

2. Paul Schullery. 2002. Lewis and Clark Among the Grizzlies: Legend and Legacy in the American West. Falcon. An Imprint of the Globe Pequod Press. Helena Montana.
3. Kerry A. Gunther. 1991. Grizzly bear activity and human-induced modifications in Pelican Valley, Yellowstone National Park. M. S. Thesis, Montana State University.

Chapter 20. Bear-Viewing Takes Flight

1. Government of British Columbia. 1995. Grizzly Bear Conservation in BC: Background Report. (p. 57).
2. David J. Mattson, BM Blanchard and RR Knight. 1992. Yellowstone Grizzly Bear Mortality, Human Habituation, and Whitebark Pine Seed Crops. J. of Wildlife Management. Vol. 56, No. 3, (p. 432-442).

Chapter 21: Hunting the Great Bear: The Crossroads of Biology, Ethics, and Management

1. Katherine Ringsmuth, *At the Heart of Katmai: An Administrative History of the Brooks River Area, with Special Emphasis on Bear Management in Katmai National Park and Preserve 1912–2006*, (National Park Service, 2013).

Chapter 22: Wild Bears or Industrial-strength Tourism?

1. George Catlin, *Illustrations of the Manners, Customs and Conditions of the North American Indians*, (London: Dover Publications, 1848).

   "... imagine them as they might in future be seen (by some great protecting policy of government preserved in their pristine beauty and wildness, in a magnificent park, where the world could see for ages to come, the native Indian in his classic attire .... A nation's Park containing man and beast amid all the wild and freshness of nature's beauty."

Chapter 23: Bears Are Like Us: Restoring Their Future

1. K.A. Blecha, R.B. Boone, and M.W. Alldredge, "Hunger mediates apex predator's risk avoidance response in wildland-urban interface," *Journal of Animal Ecology* 87 (2008): 609–622.

Chapter 24: Do's and Don'ts in Grizzly Country

1. Katherine Ringsmuth, *At the Heart of Katmai: An Administrative History of the Brooks River Area, with Special Emphasis on Bear Management in Katmai National Park and Preserve 1912–2006*, (National Park Service, 2013).

   > "Many times, a bear walking down the beach has been forced to change direction due to a line of people with flashing cameras in front of the lodge, appearing to the bear as an obstacle. Behind the bear is usually a line of floatplanes parked on the beach, which creates a similar obstacle. Ultimately the direction the bear takes is right into camp."

2. Elliott Coues, ed., *The History of the Lewis and Clark Expedition*, (New York: Dover Publications, Inc., 1979).
3. Reuben Gold Thwaites, *Original Journals of the Lewis and Clark Expedition 1804–1806*, (New York: Antiquarian Press Ltd., 1959).

Chapter 25: Stories Out There of a Changed Bear

1. Adolph Murie, *The Grizzlies of Mount McKinley*. (Seattle: University of Washington Press, 1981).
2. Marc Cattet, J. Boulanger, G. Stenhouse, R. A. Powell, and M.J. Reynolds, "An Evaluation of Long-Term Capture Effects in Ursids: Implications for Wildlife Welfare and Research," *Journal of Mammalogy* 89(4) (2008): 973–990.

About the Author

Born in Kingston, Ontario, Barrie Gilbert graduated with a degree in biology from Queen's University, going on to earn a PhD in zoology from Duke University. After a stint as an Alberta wildlife research biologist, he joined the faculty of Utah State University, where he taught courses on animal behavior, wildlife management and endangered species. His research interests include human-wildlife interactions, especially the three species of North American bears; studies of dolphin communication; and ungulate behavior. Since retiring, Dr. Gilbert has focused on bringing ecological insights to conservation of threatened species and habitats. His hobbies include photography, sailing, mountain biking, and physical fitness.

CPSIA information can be obtained
at www.ICGtesting.com
Printed in the USA
LVHW010424160120
643424LV00004B/47